PUBS and PINTS

The Story of Luton's
Public Houses and Breweries

Stuart Smith

The
Book
Castle

First published September 1995
by
The Book Castle
12 Church Street
Dunstable
Bedfordshire LU5 4RU

ISBN 1 871199 72 7 (hardback)
ISBN 1 871199 97 2 (paperback)

Computer typeset by Keyword, Aldbury, Hertfordshire.
Printed in Great Britain by the Antony Rowe Ltd., Chippenham, Wiltshire.

CONTENTS

Preface

This book stems from my long interest in local history and my desire to produce a 'theme' publication. I have an extensive collection of photographs showing all aspects of Luton's changing facade, especially since the end of the last war, and having considered the number of licenced premises that have disappeared for one reason or another or have been extensively rebuilt, it occurred to me that a photographic record of these lost 'watering holes' would add to the published local history store.

Certainly the number of licenced public houses has declined from a high of one hundred and twenty years ago. William Austin, in his 'History of Luton', recorded that, in 1871, there were 269 licenced houses in the town, one for every seventy-seven inhabitants or one for every forty-eight persons over the age of thirteen. Compare these figures to the present time when the total number of public houses in Luton including its hamlets of Stopsley, Leagrave, Limbury and Biscot stands at 101, which includes two that are currently closed and facing doubtful futures. This number does not take into account all of the off-licence premises, of which there are many. Even with the decline in the numbers of public houses the age old tradition is in little danger of disappearing completely, as the English, in the nicest sense of the word, are drinking men and hold the pub in high esteem.

The brewing and retail trade are both undergoing constant change. Public houses bought or leased from the brewers seem to have name changes once a week, and the large breweries are constantly exchanging licenced premises between themselves. Since the advent of the Mergers and Monopolies Commission, it has become difficult to keep track of public house ownership. 'Inn Business', for instance, are a totally independant company and have a firm foothold in the town. They lease public houses from a variety of brewers, free from tie, and then rent to the tenants. They then buy their beer and supplies from any brewery they wish, depending on price and quality of beer. At present, Inn Business own five public houses in Luton: *The Chequers, The Inkerman Arms, The Melson, The Railway Tavern* and *The Old English Gentleman*.

Since I started to research information for this book no less than ten pubs have changed their names and there have been four name changes while the manuscript was being typed. I am quite sure that between the time of going for publication and appearing in print, there will be more name changes and possibly breweries changing hands. I have not made distinctions between 'tenant' and 'manager' and where the terms are used they are meant to indicate the occupier.

No detailed account has been included dealing with off-licences, although I have included photographs of several of the more prominent outlets. From 1834 on-licences and off-licences were issued separately, the main requests for off-licences being from grocers as they were able to deliver beer, wines and spirits to the gentry and the new middle classes with their weekly orders. In recent years there has been an increase in off-sales outlets, including the traditional off-licence, corner grocer shop and the ubiquitous supermarket. These reflect the change in customer drinking habits, where having a drink round the television or video is preferable to the pleasure of using a local public house, whether it be because of the reduction in potency of the drink, its increased cost or the dangers of drinking and driving, hence the cost of a taxi fare.

The photographs used cover about one hundred years of Luton's recent history and I hope that this pictorial record will be of interest to Lutonians old and new. Some of the dates quoted have been estimated and I would be grateful for any comments and information from readers, and the opportunity to copy old photographs that are relevant would be welcomed. Photographic sources are individually credited where due. Those without credit are from my own collection.

For readers who are new to the town or are not old enough to remember the location of many of the public houses, I have used street diagrams to indicate their position. The maps used are, of course, relevant to the time that the buildings in question were standing.

The section dealing with the Breweries that have had a foothold in the town has been presented in alphabetical order, except for the Breweries of Burr, Sworder, J. W. Green, Flowers and Whitbread, which have been handled as one group, the reason being that they have all, at one time or another, operated as Luton's 'own' brewery.

I wish to take this opportunity to thank the many people who have given great assistance and advice in the preparation of the book, including the staff of Luton Central Library, Dr. Elizabeth Adey and the staff of Luton Museum and Art Gallery, The Luton News and its photographers, The Evening Post-Echo. Dr Stephen Bunker of the University of Luton, Ken Cooper, Terry Hyde, Ken Page of Greene King Brewery, Benskins Brewery, Tony Hill of Charles Wells Brewery, Mr Monckton, Mr Armitage and Nick Redman of Whitbread Archive, Ken Thomas of Courage Archive, Ken Smith (formally of Benskins Brewery), David White for much help with the photography, Dennis Ruttledge of McMullen and Sons, David Wiseman, Colin Glover for coming up trumps with many of my 'missing' photographs, Phil Eversden for some useful hints and contacts, Catherine Peddar, Barry Allen, Stuart Goodyear, David Kilby, Michael Allen, David Craddock, Peter Christeas and his staff at Snappy Snaps, and to all my other friends and colleagues who have shown an interest and added snippets and ideas over the years.

Amongst secondary sources I am conscious of having shamelessly gleaned from the work of fellow historians William Austin, Vic Lea, John Ramm, Helen Poole, Ken Page and C. J. Peaple. I am grateful to them for this help. My thanks go also to all the landlords and landladies whose beer I have partaken and whose help and information I have gladly received.

Naturally my greatest debt is to my wife Phyl, who always believed in the book, and to my children Kirsty and Lyndsey, who must have thought, at times, that their father had taken root at his computer. This book is for them, and for Patricia Minihane and my parents, who would have loved to read it.

Introduction

The majority of people in Luton, if asked the question, 'What industry or trade has been the mainstay of Luton's development over the years?' most probably would answer 'the hat industry' followed closely by 'engineering and in particular the motor industry'. These answers would not be incorrect, as they have both been instrumental in the development of present day Luton, but perhaps, along with farming and agriculture, the main continuous trade carried out in south Bedfordshire and notably Luton is the brewing and sale of beer and spirits.

The work of straw plaiting and the making of straw hats has been carried on in south Bedfordshire and in Luton and its hamlets of Stopsley, Leagrave, Limbury and East and West Hyde for around three hundred years. A petition presented to Parliament on behalf of the inhabitants of south Bedfordshire in 1689 claimed that 14,000 people were dependent on the straw hat industry as their sole means of income. Plaiting and the finishing of straw hats was, on the whole, a cottage industry and financially very rewarding for the straw hat businessmen.

Engineering and the motor industry, by comparison, are a much more recent addition to our history, only appearing and coming to the fore in the last one hundred years. It was after 1876, when Luton became a borough, that the leading businessmen in the town, who were in the main members of the Chamber of Commerce and also town councillors, decided that they were responsible for the future development of the town. In 1889 discussions led to the formation of the New Industries Committee. The task of this committee was to try and encourage new firms, not connected to hat making, to move to Luton where land was plentiful and electricity cheap. Over the next twenty years businesses, which were to change the economic face of Luton and become major employers, were to come and settle. These included such names as Haywood Tyler, Laportes, CWS Cocoa Works, Commercial Cars (later Commer), Davies Gas Stove Company, George Kents, SKF Ball Bearings and of course Vauxhall Motors.

The history of brewing goes back much further, in fact it was about six thousand years ago when barley was first malted and fermented in the Middle East. There is abundant evidence that the secret of brewing was known to the Assyrians and ancient Egyptians. From Julius Caesar and other authors, it is clear that a form of ale was also drunk by the German tribes facing the legionairies across the northernmost frontiers of the Roman Empire. In Britain, the drinking of ale made from barley is recorded as early as the first century, AD. Pliny the Elder wrote about the Western nations 'intoxicating themselves with moistened grain'.

The Romans disliked ale and the traditional British drink of cider and so shipped in their own wine and eventually planted their own vineyards. It was the Anglo Saxons who popularised the drinking of ale and this continued until the Norman invasion when another change back to wine, for the Normans at least, took place. The Saxon peasants in general still brewed their ale, which gave rise to a type of class distinction which was to last for many hundreds of years.

In the fifteenth century brewing was already well established in Luton and Austin recounts that in 1474 Luton had at least sixty malt kilns. Some of this malting took place in taverns but a great deal was carried out on farms, the source of water being the River Lea. Despite the popularity of the end product the brewer was not considered to be a prominent citizen and didn't feature high on the social scale; indeed, much of the brewing was often carried out by the farmer's or innkeeper's wife. The monasteries were also large suppliers of ale having developed great skills in brewing. It was the dissolution of the monasteries that led to a steep rise in the art of commercial brewing.

The traditional English ale of this time was generally of a sweet taste but since 1524 when many Flemish immigrants came to this country with their own ideas of using hops to flavour their 'bierre' the taste buds of the ale drinking population gradually changed to accept the new bitter beers introduced by the refugees. The old sweet ales still continued to be brewed and it was more than one hundred years before they finally died out.

Towards the end of the sixteenth century the main occupations of the townspeople were farming and brewing. Spirits made from fermented cereals or potatoes were freely available and on sale practically everywhere, while beer cost 1s 10d a barrel, (9p in today's coinage).

The first recorded mention of beer in bottles, in any substantial quantity, was made in 1676 when a local brewer, George Cross, supplied the Russell family with ten and one half barrels to be bottled 'for my lord's drinking'. By modern standards this amount was negligible, and it was over two hundred years before beer in bottles was to make its mark on the English drinking habits. Part of the reason for this being that from the beginning of the eighteenth century it was illegal for beer to be sold other than in mugs or tankards officially stamped and measured.

The late seventeenth century saw the growth of the brewer who supplied several inns with his product. These brewers were generally farmers who had been brewing to supply their estates, and innkeeper brewers who had for whatever reasons become more successful than their neighbour brewers. Great names such as Courage and Truman appeared at about this time.

These common brewers soon realised that they could make greater profits and stabilise their sales if they also owned the beer outlets and it is from this period that the practice of tied houses began. Many innkeepers continued to brew on their premises as did many farms and estates and it wasn't until 1887 that the Truck Amendments Act made it illegal for employers to pay their workers beer in kind. This Act led to many estate and private breweries closing down as the brewer's licence of 40 shillings was still due. Many of the licensed breweries started to amalgamate at this time and the records show that the number of breweries nationally of 135,000 in 1870 had decreased to 9,600 by 1890.

The eighteenth century and the early nineteenth century saw the rivalry for the title of the national drink between beer and gin, indeed many beerhouses were dubbed 'gin palaces' after witnessing many abusers ravaged by the demon spirit. The Temperance Movement began to take a hold, often organising marches and demonstrations outside these 'evil dens of iniquity' and regaling the customers as to the error of their ways, and more often than not receiving in return certain derogatory remarks.

On her accession, Queen Victoria became the patron of the British and Foreign Temperance Society. A few years later, in 1850, 'total abstinence' was urged as a stimulant to a dying cause. The following year, the Band of Hope was founded for the protection of juveniles who were still permitted to frequent public houses and consume liquor on the premises. Not for nearly thirty years would this be forbidden to children under thirteen years of age, from which figure it advanced to the present age limit of eighteen. In 1852, the teaching of temperance was introduced in the curriculum of most schools, which were, in most cases, run by the churches.

One year later, the United Kingdom Alliance sought 'to procure the total and immediate legislative suppression of the traffic in intoxicating liquors and beverages'. The formation of the Church of England Temperance Society in 1862 brought the largest force organised so far in the cause of teetotalism. A National Prohibition Party founded a few years later represented the extreme section of the movement.

The seventies revealed a greater consumption of alcohol of all kinds than ever before. In 1874, for instance, the average per head was thirty-six gallons, or one barrel of beer, and this despite the rapidly diminishing number of public houses.

During the last quarter of the nineteenth century some of the great brewing families came to the fore, among those being Whitbread, Worthington, Bass and Watney.

The large breweries found great success due to the increase in sales as the improving transportation channels, the railways and canals, made it easier to supply tied houses over a greater area. The opportunity to export their products followed with the export trade in beer to India being an outstanding success. India Pale Ale was specifically developed to suit the hot climate.

The twentieth century saw the big brewing mergers take place and brewing is now mostly in the hands of Whitbread, Watney Truman (owned by Grand Metropolitan and Courage), Scottish and Newcastle, Bass Charrington, and Allied Breweries.

With the peace that arrived after the first war, came longer opening hours – although the abnormally long hours worked by publicans would never return – renewed supplies of raw materials and, most important of all, a general desire to recover lost ground. The 'Improved Public House' movement shelved for so long, could now go forward as a long-term policy. For the first few months after the war it was mainly the task of brewers to set their houses in order before beginning to improve them. That done, they could examine the general position and select those premises which were best tackled first.

The first inns in England were opened by, or for, the Romans hence one of the commonest signs – *The Chequers*. Chess was a popular game in Rome and those inns or taverns where it could be played would advertise the fact by displaying a real or painted chequer board on the exterior wall or door of the building. The Romans continued this practice in England hence the profusion of this public house name. There is one house in Luton bearing this ancient name. Another inn sign dating back to the Romans is *The Bush*. The sign for a tabernae was in the form of a bundle of grapevine leaves hung on a chain on the outside wall of the establishment. This indicated that new wine had been delivered and was ready for sale. Over the centuries there have been many public houses bearing this name or a derivative of it. *The Holly Bush* is a corruption of the name.

The Saxons were the first to introduce the pub sign as we now know it. They would use an 'Ale-stake', a wooden pole driven into the ground or the thatch of the roof, to show that there was ale to be purchased on the premises. They would put a bundle of leaves, as the Romans, on the end of the stake. As the house, where ale could be purchased, was identified by the ale-stake, then over a period of time it became the inn sign, with a variety of adornments hanging from it. There are several paintings, dating back to the fourteenth century, showing religious establishments with an ale-stake adorned with symbols of a golden cross and of cross keys. *The Popes Head* was very popular until Henry the Eighth broke with Rome, after which many inns featuring this sign quickly changed it to *The Kings Head*.

In 1393, King Richard the Second decreed that alehouses must have signs. He proclaimed 'Whosoever shall brew ale with the intention of selling it must hang out a sign; otherwise he shall forfeit his ale'. This was done so that the examiner or tester of ales would know the location of each public house. Therefore, from those days, public houses and their signs became synonymous. The law also decreed that when a pub lost its licence, the sign had to be taken down. A law was passed in 1375, stating that no pub should have an ale-stake or sign extending over the King's highway by more than seven feet.

The greatest influence on the modern sign was the illiteracy of the majority of the population until late in the nineteenth century. The signs therefore, began to be of a pictorial nature as well as being large, bright and relatively simple. Animals, religious symbols and heraldic arms came to the fore as did the symbols depicting the various trades.

Queen Elizabeth the First had a strong influence on the signs. She appeared on many signs during her reign but was unhappy about the likenesses. She approved of one official painting and insisted that it be copied faithfully; any other version already in place had to be taken down and destroyed.

Queen Victoria took an opposite stance and decreed that no pub sign could show a living member of royalty. The Lord Chamberlain is charged with enforcing this Act, and quite recently had to order some public houses to change their signs. This was when the Prince of Wales married Diana, and some pubs showed their sign featuring the new Princess of Wales.

The term 'public house' is quite a modern name in the history of brewing, inn or tavern being used far more frequently. Most public houses still existing date from the Victorian age and were built to serve the working community that tilled the land or moved into the towns and cities during the Industrial Revolution.

From the very early nineteenth century, purpose built public houses began to appear in ever increasing numbers in the highly populated areas. Quite often the original core fabric of these buildings still survives today. Before this building explosion, alehouses had been ordinary dwelling houses adapted, with few alterations, for the business of drinking. The purpose built houses were constructed with ground plans, fixtures, furnishings and facades suited to the victualling trade.

The rapid increase of legal and illegal beerhouses was the direct result of the 1830 Beer Act, which allowed almost any householder to sell beer provided he obtain an excise permit. The new law was celebrated up and down the country. In 1830, over 24,000 beerhouses opened their doors for the first time, and five years later the figure was around 40,000. Taken in context, this figure was about three-quarters of the number of traditional public houses.

Beerhouse premises were often small and dingy, and most often were situated in courts and alleyways. The back room of the beerhouse was the most frequent location for the serious business. The typical customer was generally of the working class and poor, and most could not afford the higher prices charged in the publican's tap room. In addition, the beerhouse offered some services to the labourer which the respectable public house had come to neglect. They were places for gaming, finding jobs and lodgings, picking up prostitutes, organising petty crimes and for fencing stolen goods. They were also the scene of many drunken fist fights. Overall, the beershop seems to have occupied part of the social territory which the alehouse or public house had vacated since becoming more respectable with the turn of the new century.

The 'pub' as we know it has become the centre of social life, even though of late, the 'Drink but don't drive' campaign has adversely affected the number of clientele, and hence the profits that the archetypal English pub once enjoyed. To try and combat this loss in revenue many of the small pubs now provide meals and snacks as a matter of course and put on entertainment such as music and quizzes to attract, or keep, a regular customer base. The majority of publicans' trade comes from the eighteen to thirty year old public and this fraternity can be very choosy about the 'in place' to drink, and once the choice is made as to which pub is 'in', the publican can expect a huge rise in trade with a busy but comfortable few years ahead of him. Unfortunately, when the mood takes them and a different watering hole is desired, this transient group of drinkers tends to want a change in environment and word gets around, when a different pub can expect its trade to boom for a while. The major breweries are aware of this trend and strive to attract these very mobile consumers by redecorating their houses into various 'theme pubs'; some are successful, others not.

In the meantime many typical corner pubs carry on with a regular clientele where traditional pub games of darts, dominoes, crib and sometimes skittles are played, and they offer a welcome respite from the queues, stepped-on-toes and spilled beer that sometimes happen in a crowded town centre theme pub. Each of these establishments serves a purpose and gives the customer what he or she wants, namely good conversation, good company and above all good refreshment.

Malting, Brewing and Transportation

In order to understand the part that barley plays in the malting process, it is necessary to realise that malting is, to a great extent, a speeded-up process of what goes on when barley is planted in the ground. When the barley is planted, it is necessary to have a certain amount of moisture present before the barley will start to germinate. This moisture, provided temperatures are suitable, excites germination, so that the germ or embryo starts to develop rudimentary rootlets and shoots. Obviously the germ has to obtain nutrition in order to do this, and it does so by sending out enzymes or agents which prepare the starch and protein into suitable forms of food for the young plant. When the roots are well established and the shoot is above the ground, there is practically nothing left of the original barleycorn, except the husk.

The following processes were the age old traditional stages of taking the raw materials and producing beer. These operations were carried out in maltings and breweries for over two hundred years by armies of brewery workers and brewers until the advent of automation, when many of the processes are started, controlled and ended by the push of a button, usually by the master brewer. Automation or not, the processes described are still very necessary in the production of beer, it's just that the manual and visual input is not always apparent.

The following descriptions of the malting and brewing processes are as were carried out in the Luton Brewery of J. W. Green during the 1950s, but the identical processes would have been carried out in the hundreds of breweries the length and breadth of the country.

In the maltings, the maltster makes use of this natural process, but in such a manner as to have it under very accurate control. All the maltster wants to do is to develop the barley, which when received from the farmer is hard and vitreous, and quite incapable of yielding an extract by normal brewing methods, in such a manner as will enable it to be used in the brewery mash tuns.

The methods used by the maltsters in imitation of nature are, first of all to soak or steep the barley in water for a period of about sixty hours. The water used is at or about the normal tap water temperature. When the steeping period is over, the barley, which has been drained clear of water, is dropped to the floor below the steeping cistern. Here it is spread out in a thick and even layer, which stretches from one side of the malthouse floor almost to the other. Here the barley is left for a period which may vary from twelve to forty-eight hours according to the temperature of the air, after which time it shows signs of sprouting.

7

This is a critical stage in the malting process, and part of the art of malting is from now on to control the temperature of the growing barley with the greatest care. This is done by hand turning and spreading the barley evenly out on the floors of the malthouse. Various types of shovels and forks are used for the purpose of turning the barley, according to the stage the process has reached. Most of these are of a wooden construction so as to avoid damage to the growing barley.

Briefly, the process of flooring or growing the barley goes on for about ten days, during which time the individual floors of growing barley are thickened up and thinned out, turned and ploughed according to how the growth is proceeding and the temperature of each particular piece. Twelve to fourteen days after steeping, the barley has rootlets of anything up to half an inch long, and the corn itself is quite soft, so much so that it is fairly easy to crumble it between index finger and thumb of one's hand. Indeed this is a commonly applied test to know whether the green malt, as it is then called, is ready for going to the kiln.

All that the maltster has so far done is to allow the natural agents present in the barleycorn to attack the cellulose skins of the starch cells, thereby leaving the starch in the interior of these cells available for conversion into malt sugars during the mashing processes in the brewery. It is most important that the maltster should not proceed further at this stage, for this would lead to waste of raw material. In fact, all the maltster really has to do is pave the way for the extract to be taken from the starch without using too much of that material for the purpose of the growth of the plant.

Kilning is the process which the maltster uses to bring matters to a standstill as far as germination is concerned, but without destroying the natural agents which are present in the region of the germ, and which are later required to convert the reserve food store into sweet wort in the brewing process. The art of kilning consists of cautiously drying the malt to a stage known as hand dry, and then gradually raising the temperature to a point where further germination is prevented and the malt at the same time acquires the 'biscuity' malty flavour which is its characteristic.

A kiln is a tall building with a large ventilator on top of a tapering roof. Inside the building and just below the roof level is a large stainless steel wire floor of such a mesh as will prevent the germinated barley falling through, but which will at the same time allow air from below to pass through. Below the wire floor is the furnace which heats the air, and the baffles which spread the air evenly. The furnace is fired by the purest anthracite so as to avoid smoke.

This process of kilning enables the moisture content to be kept very low, which is very important in connection with the efficient storage of malt. Before being despatched to the brewery, all malt is stored in special bins, and in such a manner as will keep its moisture content as low as possible. The malt is always stored with the rootlets on. During

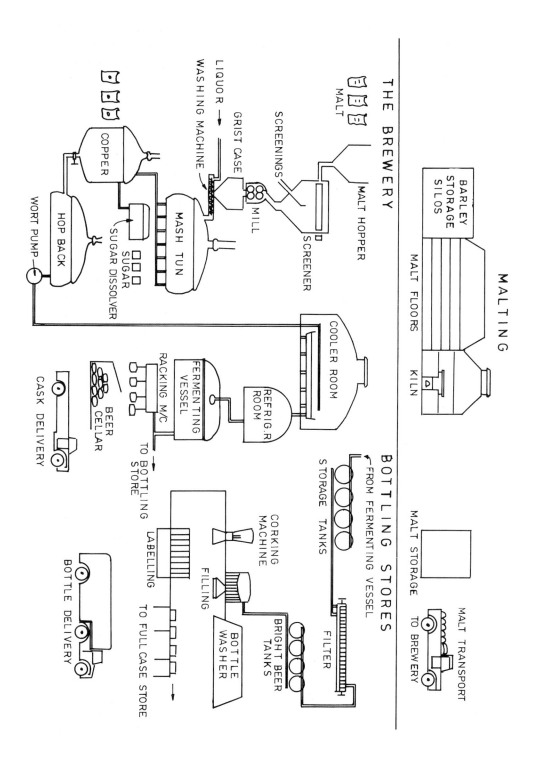

kilning these rootlets turn a reddish-brown colour and become very dry and brittle, and the reason for storing them with the malt is that they pick up moisture more readily than malt does, and as afterwards they are screened away from the malt, their presence during storage is helpful. Malt culm (the rootlets) is the main by-product of malting and is in great demand for use as meal for livestock.

On arrival at the brewery, the malt is screened and polished and fed to a special type of roller mill, which cracks the grain without unduly crushing it. It would be quite wrong to grind the malt into a fine powder since the husk performs a very important function during part of the process, and excessive crushing or grinding would also lead to the extraction of materials which are undesirable from the brewer's point of view. After being suitably crushed, the malt drops into what is known as the grist case. Here it lies until it is required for brewing.

At 5am on the morning of a brewing day a brewer will be on duty ready to start off the process of brewing. Prior to his arrival, a number of men will have been engaged in raising steam pressure in the boiler house, and heating a number of water tanks or liquor tanks as they are called in the brewery. Water is never referred to as such in a brewery, but it is always known as 'hot liquor' or 'cold liquor'. Using the term 'water' would be liable to incur a fine of a gallon of beer!

The mash tun will have been heated to the correct temperature and everything will be ready for what is known as mashing, a very important stage in the art, craft and mystery of brewing. With everything in order, the brewer opens up the hot liquor valves which feed the mashing machine and simultaneously opens the slide at the bottom of the grist case, so that the crushed malt drops through and is mixed with the hot liquor as it passes through the mashing machine. This machine is really a cylinder fitted internally with an Archimedean screw and beaters.

The mixed crushed malt and liquor emerges in a porridgy mass and enters the mash tun. The process of mashing takes about twenty minutes, and the brewer's skill comes into operation in seeing that the temperatures of the liquor are just right, and that the amount of liquor used is of the correct proportions. When all the malt has been mashed, the mash tun will be found to contain a floating mass, known to brewers as the 'mash' or 'goods'. So accurate and skilful is the manipulation of this process that the final temperatures are gauged to plus or minus one degree, and the amount of liquor used is gauged to a matter of a gallon or two.

The mash is then rested for a period at one temperature, and then brought up or down in temperature for different periods of time according to what the brewer wishes to bring about. About two hours after mashing, all the readily available extract from the original reserve food store is converted into what is known as malt wort, a syrupy liquid with a very pronounced sweet malty taste.

From the mash tun, the malt wort is taken to the coppers in which it is boiled. The spent mash now only consists of grains which are unsuitable for further use in brewing, but nevertheless make first class feeding stuff for cattle, and is in ready demand by farmers.

Whilst the wort is running from the mash tun to the copper it is usual in breweries to add a certain amount of cane sugar. This is first dissolved by steam before adding to the copper. To achieve the bitter flavour of beer, hops are added to the mixture in the copper where the whole is boiled for up to a couple of hours. The mixture then goes to the hop back where the spent hops are removed from the boiled wort, after which it is then pumped right to the top of the brewery on to the coolers, where it remains for a short period in shallow copper vessels and in an atmosphere of pure air.

From the coolers the wort proceeds to the refrigerator room where it is cooled before passing to the fermenting vessels, where it is gauged for Excise purposes, and where yeast is added to it in order to bring about the process of fermentation.

Fermenting vessels are usually completely filled with the day's brewing at about 5pm in the evening. At this time the Excise man steps forward and gauges the strength of the wort or sugar solution, which is just about to undergo fermentation. Furthermore, he calculates the quantity that is present and thus arrives at his charge for duty.

The actual process of the main fermentation goes on for about a week, after which it is racked in casks or tanks which have been scalded out with boiling water and steam, and have been inspected to make sure they are in every way fit for the storage of beer. Towards the end of the process, the surplus yeast, which is thrown up to the surface, is skimmed away from the beer and taken to a cold room, where it is kept for further use.

A certain amount of dry hops is added to these casks, so as to give flavour to the finished beer. Sometimes during racking draught beer a small quantity of priming is added. This is a sugar solution used to induce the yeast remaining in the beer to carry on a slow and steady fermentation whilst the beer is being matured in the wood, if intended for draught purposes, or in a tank if required for bottling. The actual maturation period of the beer depends on the type of beer being produced.

The beer for bottling travels to storage tanks and then to bright beer tanks via a filter. The gas present in bottled beer is natural and is generated by the remaining yeast in the beer. The washed bottles, after filling, capping and labelling are then, along with the cask beer, ready for delivery to the licenced outlet.

There are many different types of beer. Mild beer is sweet and milder in flavour than bitter beer, which has a pleasant appetising bitter flavour. A light coloured bitter beer requires to be brewed from the highest quality malt and needs more and better quality hops than with mild beer. All beers can be divided into categories of dry, medium and sweet. Dry drinking beers have from time immemorial been regarded as the highest quality beers. Dry beers are almost invariably those brewed from a high proportion of malt. Colour in beer means nothing, except in the case of strong beer, which is impossible to brew at a light colour owing to the high concentration of malt which is used.

The main hop-growing areas are Kent, Worcestershire and Hereford-shire and the harvesting time for the ripe hops is the late summer. The traditional working holiday for hundreds of East London families would be in September when they would descend on the hop farms of Kent for the duration of the harvest where they would eat, sleep and work in the open air to earn their money.

The gathered hops would be laid on an open griddled floor above a kiln for drying. After cooling they would be packed into sacks and delivered to the breweries.

The end product of all these raw materials and complex processes had to be transported to the public houses, and the brewing trade have been responsible for the introduction of many odd and unusual vehicles to carry out this task. In the days when a brewhouse supplied only a few local pubs, the easiest and most convenient way of delivering a barrel would be to have a cask slung beneath a yoke carried on the shoulders of two men. As the Common Brewer came to the fore with the takeover of other brewhouses further afield, a more efficient method of carriage was required. The obvious transport was two and four wheeled horse drawn farm wagons and these were in use for the better part of a century.

The many breweries centred around Burton on Trent developed a distinctive cart with a low slung chassis, making the loading of heavy casks much easier. Bass Charrington still operate motorised drays with air suspension which when in its static condition allows the chassis to ride at a low accessible height. By the end of the nineteenth century steam driven waggons capable of carrying heavy loads were in use with breweries, and were to remain in use until the 1930s. The two and four horse drays remained in service well into the 1950s, particularly for local deliveries. Many breweries still maintain several dray horses for use on special occasions and for shows and exhibitions.

Rail transportation and petrol and diesel trucks now dominate the dray scene and are unlikely to be superseded in the forseeable future. Electric delivery lorries were pioneered by Whitbread during the inter war years and both Ind Coope and Watney's experimented with two and three wheeled scooter vehicles, although these were mainly for advertising and promotional purposes.

BREWERIES SERVING LUTON

Breweries Located Within Luton

BURR: SWORDER: GREEN: FLOWER: WHITBREAD

The main supplier of beer and spirits to the public house trade in modern Luton is Whitbread plc, but this firm's dominance as a supplier to the town has been for a comparatively short time. The chain of events started with a small Luton inn nearly 350 years ago. Its name was *The Wheelplough* and it stood on the east side of Park Street approximately under what is now the flyover bridge. What this small town inn had in common with many others at the time was that at the rear of the building were facilities for malting and brewing. It was first mentioned in 1655 when James Wilkins, a Wheathampstead brewer, purchased the property for £40. His master brewer was a man called Robert Parrott and he converted a cottage at the rear of the inn for Mr Parrott to ply his trade. Within the year the two men became partners.

With many inns brewing their own beer the success of any particular establishment rested with the master brewer. Robert Parrott must have been one of the best because the *Wheelplough* brewery thrived and

The White House; home of the Burr family. The house was demolished in 1908.

13

remained in the ownership of the Wilkins family for 165 years. The family finally sold out in 1820 to Solomon Burr for the sum of £995 and an annuity of £250 for twenty years. Not a bad return for the initial purchase price of £40.

Solomon Burr came from a family of Luton landowners and brewers. He and his brother already operated a brewery behind their substantial house on Park Square. The house was commonly known as the White House and stood where what is now the front entrance gate to the University of Luton. It had been built in 1767 and first started brewing in the name of Edmund Humphrey. Upon his retirement in 1776 he moved to a large house in George Street and sold his house and brewery to Thomas Godfrey Burr, also a brewer. Upon his death in 1798 the business passed to his widow and two sons, William and Jonathan. By 1811 William ran the whole concern and was then succeeded by Solomon and William's sons Frederick and Charles.

The White House was demolished in 1908 to make way for the building of Luton Modern School, which in turn was demolished in 1957 and replaced by the present buildings. After the brewery was closed, the buildings were divided up, with the Dye Works of Carruthers taking over some of the site, and the Luton Reporter newspaper occupying the old brewery offices. The malting rooms continued to be operated by Thomas Sworder to keep his Anchor Brewery supplied with the basic materials for brewing.

The Wheelplough continued to operate as an inn but the Burr family closed the malting and brewery to concentrate their business at Park Square on the site of the old Humphrey brewery.

Brewers, in general, were facing stiff competition and sought to secure as many independent inns under their banner as possible. The Burrs held several houses in and around Luton with the old coaching inn, *The Cock*, which stood opposite their brewery being the jewel in the crown.

Good water is essential in the production of good beer and all the breweries sought a clean reliable source of this precious commodity. The Burrs sank a new well on the site of the Park Square brewery and proudly boasted the fact that its depth of five hundred feet, unheard of until then, was an indication as to the lengths they would go to provide their customers with the best brew possible. In 1834, with some of the clay from the deepest part of the well, master brewer Frederick Burr had a ceremonial brick made, duly named and dated, and personally laid the brick in the wall of *The Cock Inn*.

From the time when the brewer was considered fairly low on the social scale he had now reached greater heights, so much so that the master brewer was the highest paid artisan in the town. Certainly, in the brewery, his word was law and it would take a brave man to cross him. His skill and secrets of fine brewing were in great demand and his influence reached beyond the walls of his workplace. An interesting incident occurred in 1830 to reinforce this fact. The master brewer for the Burr family at this time was Charles Burr and he asked the churchwardens of St. Mary's parish church if they would move the clock, which was on the north face of the tower facing Church Street, to the west face so that it would look onto the brewery yard. He reasoned that it would be of great service to himself and his employees. The request was met and the change made.

As mentioned earlier, the Burr family were also noted landowners and a large piece of Burge Field in High Town formed part of the Burr estate. This piece of land covered the area now enclosed by Burr Street, York Street, Back Street and Hitchin Road. Historian Frederick Davis records that one of the charities registered in the town was from the estate of the late Frederick Burr. It stated that 'the profits of seven acres in Burge Field, High Town, were to be distributed to the poor on St. Thomas's Day each year'.

As parcels of their land were sold off for building purposes the family were honoured and remembered by having some of the streets named

The old brewery yard, Park Square. c. 1898. Originally the home of E. Humphrey's brewery, followed by the Burr family's brewery. It can be seen how clearly the church clock is visible to brewery workers after being moved at the request of Charles Burr, Master Brewer. (courtesy: Ken Cooper)

The Burr family tomb in the Parish Church cemetery.

after family members, hence: Burr Street, Charles Street, Reginald Street and Frederick Street.

In 1857, Burrs brewery was sold along with all its inns, taverns and hotels including the old *Wheelplough* to Thomas Sworder of Hertford for the sum of £41,250. The Park Square brewery buildings survived for some years before their demolition.

The Burr family tomb was situated in the church grounds just outside the Burr's property boundary and can be seen today very close to the rear wall of the University, the boundary lines remaining as they were.

There were other independent maltsters and brewers operating at this time, amongst those being William Adams, who in 1796 built his malting and brewhouse to the rear of the buildings on the west side of Park Square. The site of his business premises was adjacent to the site of what was to become the Phoenix Brewery of J. W. Green. To the rear of the properties on the corner of Chapel Street and George Street, on the site now covered by the Westminster Bank, John Anstee ran a small brewery. He would later join with Thomas Sworder in a business venture when Sworder's Brewery was having some financial problems.

Thomas Sworder was not new to the town, having arrived in Luton in 1848, from his birthplace of Westmill Bury, Buntingford, Hertford-shire. He was born in 1823, and after his education at King's School, Canterbury, he joined his uncle, Mr Thomas Sworder, in the firm of solicitors, Longmore, Sworder and Longmore. Shortly after coming to the town he married, in September 1851, the eldest daughter of a very prominent man in the Luton hat industry, Mr Richard Vyse of Holly Lodge, Castle Street.

Sworder continued to practice as a solicitor for several years before reluctantly giving up his profession to take over the Bedford Road Brewery. The Crown and Anchor Brewery had been purchased at

The Bedford Road Brewery when it was purchased in 1849.
(courtesy: Bedfordshire County Record Office) (Ref. X95 / 247 & 248)

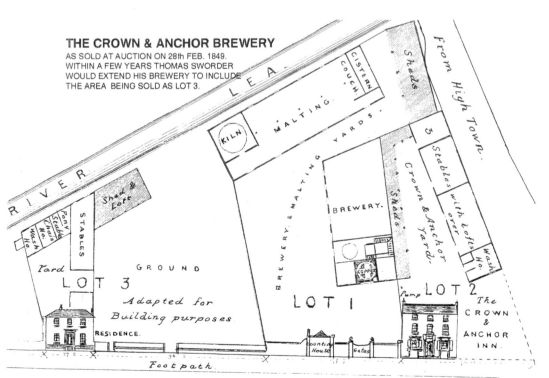

THE CROWN & ANCHOR BREWERY

AS SOLD AT AUCTION ON 28th FEB. 1849.
WITHIN A FEW YEARS THOMAS SWORDER
WOULD EXTEND HIS BREWERY TO INCLUDE
THE AREA BEING SOLD AS LOT 3.

(courtesy: Bedfordshire County Record Office) (Ref. X95/247 & 248)

auction in 1849 from Gray and Co., most probably by Thomas Sworder's brothers, Charles and Robert. Within a few years, the business appears to have been in some trouble, and Thomas made his sacrifice in order to rescue the brewery and put it on a firm footing. He quickly turned it into profitability and expanded the site northwards to cover most of the site now occupied by the Bridge Street car park, and soon to be Luton's new entertainment complex.

As well as the purchase of Burr's Brewery, he also purchased the *Albion* public house opposite his brewery on the corner of Manchester Street and Inkerman Street. There he established a mineral water factory at the rear of the public house.

He had been busy buying up many inns and his financial resources were stretched to the limit on purchase of the Burr's Park Square brewery, and more problems were on the way when inns and taverns began to suffer due to a slump in trade when the railways started to take business away from the roads. To help save his livelihood Thomas Sworder entered into an agreement with two other brewers, Bennett's of Dunstable and John Anstee who ran a small brewery behind the Westminster bank in George Street. This agreement enabled him to gain new outlets for his product and his business survived.

He also founded the Luton Wine Company and the building still remains today at the bottom of Castle Street.

At the time that Thomas Sworder was creating the Luton Wine Company a young brewer, by the name of John William Green, was starting up in business. He was born on 17th March 1847, the son of a Quaker, and they had a great effect on the economic development of the town. The Quakers, generally, were the merchants of the town and one family, the Browns, were the biggest corn millers. One of the Browns joined forces with a fellow Quaker, in 1840, to form Brown and Green, an engineering firm which specialised in making bicycles, baths, lamp posts and anything else made from iron. It was the son of the Green of the firm who in 1869 took to brewing.

The young John William Green benefitted from the will of his grandfather, John Foster, a noted Quaker minister, who died in 1864. With the legacy he began to build a highly successful brewing business, renouncing his Quaker and Liberal roots for the Conservative Party and the Church of England. In 1869, he purchased the Phoenix Brewery which had been built by Messrs. Henry and Frederick Pearman.

They had inherited a fortune from their father, Daniel Pearman, a wine merchant, who had died in 1857. The brothers indulged themselves in the good life, squandering the legacy within a generation by building a brewery situated behind Castle Street and Park Street, on land previously used for the tipping of rubbish. They ran their brewery and a wine and spirit business as separate entities, expanding and investing in the brewing side 'regardless of cost'. By 1869, the brewery

Thomas Sworder's Crown and Anchor Brewery.
(courtesy: Luton Museum and Art Gallery)

Thomas Sworder (with cane) and some of his draymen.   *(courtesy: Ken Cooper)*

The building in which Sworder founded the Luton Wine Company.

was in financial turmoil and they sold out that part of their business to J. W. Green. An advertisement was inserted in the Luton Times newspaper during January 1869 announcing that they had disposed of their brewing business to Mr J. W. Green and trusted that the patronage hitherto bestowed upon them would be transferred to their successor. In addition, they stated that their connection with the old established firm of Pearman and Sons, Wine and Spirit Merchants, remained unaltered.

Access to the Phoenix Brewery, before Park Street West was laid out, was by a narrow road which was a continuation of Middle Row on Market Hill. The last vestiges of Middle Row still exist as the side entrance to *The Rat and Carrot* public house yard although in the last couple of years this has also been bricked off several metres into the yard.

Green later acquired the brewery of Messrs. Wadsworth and Thaire located at the rear of Seamark's premises on Market Hill. The original well of this brewery was discovered during the 1940s when building alterations were being carried out on the brewery site.

The Phoenix Brewery from Park Street West, c. 1900.   *(courtesy: Ken Cooper)*

John William Green and Thomas Sworder didn't see eye to eye, especially as Green had enticed Sworder's master brewer away from him. For many years the rivalry was very bitter with Sworder using his many outlets as his chief weapon and Green retaliating by concentrating on the quality of his brew. It was Green who came out on top and Sworder, close to bankruptcy, put his entire business of three factories, the Luton Wine Company and fifty-eight hotels, inns and taverns up for auction in 1897. To the relief of the employees and the people of Luton John W. Green bid £139,000 and was successful in buying the whole organisation. He closed the Anchor Brewery in 1899, the site being purchased by John Cumberland, who converted it into an off street cattle market.

When Sworder sold his brewing concern, he was no longer a young man, being aged seventy-four. He was a very prominent citizen of the town, involving himself in local politics, and like many brewers by this time, he was a staunch Conservative and supporter of the Church. His business ability and absolute integrity were well known but he was better remembered for his generosity and good work in connection with the

21

The Phoenix Brewery yard, c. 1900.   *(courtesy: Ken Cooper)*

the Church in Luton. He had many friends among the clergy, notably the Rev. Charles Bullock, the Rev. T. J. Lee of Christ Church, and what might be called the culminating friendship with the Vicar of Luton, the Rev. James O'Neill.

Together these two fought many a School Board battle with the Education Department. During the early 1870s, when the only schools in Luton were the old British School and the Church Schools, complaints were made that there was a shortage of school accommodation in the town. The Vicar and Mr Sworder maintained that the Church should be instrumental in providing schools and education and so they, and others, fought the question in determined fashion. The outcome of their arguments was that the Education Department became convinced that there was a sufficiency of school places. They accordingly refused to grant the request for an order for the formation of a School Board. Thereupon, the trustees of the British School closed their establishment, and in the face of such a position the Department had no alternative but to order an election, the amount of available school accommodation having been greatly reduced by this means.

The Board was duly elected in February 1874, the Vicar and Thomas Sworder, maybe with the idea of 'if you can't beat them – join them' were among the first members to be elected. They formed part of the

'Church Party' within the Board and led the contests against the rival parties on issues such as providing payment of the fees for impoverished families. Despite all of these stern clashes the School Board was instrumental in providing and improving schools to the benefit of Luton.

When Sworder first came to the town he was attached to the Parish Church, but when Christ Church was opened in 1859, he transferred to it and was a valued supporter for many years. At that time, he and his wife and large family lived at the Bury, which was in what is now called Hazelbury Crescent. He was suffering from poor hearing and left Christ Church when he found he could not hear the preacher very well. He moved to the new St. Paul's Church in New Town, of which the foundation stone was laid in August 1890.

He was then living at Holly Lodge in Castle Street. The site of his house is now covered by the bus park of the Luton Bus Company, adjacent to the Catholic Church. He took a very active part during the building of St. Paul's and contributed liberally to the funds. He worshipped at St. Paul's until around 1903 when he was stricken with illness, becoming too infirm to attend. Over the following seven years his health deteriorated until finally on 21 August 1910 he died at Holly Lodge. He was interred in the Church cemetery in Crawley Green Road, where he was laid to rest alongside his great friend, the Rev. James O'Neill. His tombstone, compared to that of J. W. Green, is very modest indeed, and unfortunately, due to weather erosion, the inscriptions are virtually impossible to read.

The grave of Thomas Sworder in the church cemetery.

He was survived by fourteen children, with two of his sons gaining some fame in their own right. His second eldest son, Dr Horace Sworder, was Medical Officer for the Borough of Luton for a term of thirty years. His house on George Street was the last privately occupied house to survive. Another son, Sydney Vyse Sworder, was an enthusiastic supporter of the Luton Town Cricket Club. He is buried alongside his father.

John William Green decided to put his faith in the skill of the master brewer and to sell only quality beer. He thrived, and over the next fifty years became one of the greatest brewing concerns in the country.

In 1936, Green's acquired the St. Albans Brewery of Adey and White Ltd. with Mr H. S. Adey joining the Board of J. W. Green Ltd., on the fusion of the Companies. He retired in 1949, being succeeded by his son-in-law, Group-Captain G. F. Macpherson.

1948 saw Green's extending its interests further afield. The important and well equipped brewing concern of E. and H. Kelsey Ltd., Tunbridge Wells, Kent, became a subsidiary of the Luton Brewery. The move represented the logical sequence which occurs when a company is producing products which are popular with the public. The Kelsey family acquired the Brewery in 1851 from Lidbetter and Newman, who in turn had taken over from Kettel's Original Brewery.

One year later, the old established and well known Brewing Company of J. and J. E. Phillips Ltd. of Royston, joined forces with J. W. Green Ltd., and the Royston Brewery, which had been in the Phillips' family since 1725, ceased to brew in January 1950. The Royston Brewery was founded c.1690 and in 1725 Robert Phillips of Radwell moved to Royston and purchased the brewery on Baldock Street. Like many brewers at this time, he was a Quaker and he also operated as a Maltster.

Before the takeover by Green's, Phillips had been one of seven breweries to approach Greene King, about 1932, with a view to amalgamation or purchase, but this had not been successful. There had also been an approach to Phillips by Wells and Winch in the late 1920s, but this too came to nothing.

At the time of the amalgamation with Green's, Phillips owned 150 public houses, and at one time they owned nineteen of the twenty-six pubs in Royston. The Phillips family retained their interest in brewing through shareholdings in J. W. Green Ltd. and Lieutenant-Colonel H. P. J. Phillips and Major E. G. M. Phillips, MC, became Directors of J. W. Green Ltd.

In August 1950, the old Sussex Brewery of George Ware and Sons Ltd., Frant, where brewing had been carried on for nearly a hundred years, joined the Green group of Breweries. The Frant Brewery was closed, and the houses supplied from the Tunbridge Wells Brewery.

Further expansion came in 1951, through the amalgamation of the Lincolnshire Brewery of Soulby, Sons and Winch Ltd. of Alford. The Company was formed in 1896 to carry on the brewing, malting and wine and spirit business which had been conducted for upwards of half a century under the style of E. H. Soulby and Sons at Alford, together with agencies at Boston, Coningsby and Louth, and the old established brewing and malting business belonging to T. M. Winch and Co., known as the Louth Brewery. Since then the Red Lion Brewery, Alford, and the Phoenix Brewery, Sleaford, were acquired.

1952 was a busy year for J. W. Green's, with the purchase of Mowbray and Co. Ltd. of Grantham and of E. K. and H. Fordham Ltd. of Ashwell. The Mowbray take-over meant the widening and consolidation of the Lincolnshire side of the business. This Company was first registered in May 1888, and took over the business of brewers and maltsters of the same name established early in the last century, together with the wine and spirit business carried on under the style of Burbridge and Hutchinson. In 1891, the brewery, maltings and houses of Redhead and Co., Grantham, were purchased, and in November 1905, the brewery and upwards of fifty licenced houses of Dawber and Co., Lincoln were acquired. In 1927 G. and H. R. Hunt's Stamford Brewery and licenced premises were purchased. During this period of expansion, 1948 to 1952, Green's holdings of licenced premises increased from three hundred to over one thousand.

The Phoenix Brewery loading bay during the 1950s.   *(courtesy: Alfred Randall)*

Green delivered his products locally using horse and dray and motor lorries. His drays were always smartly turned out and the horses well groomed and tackled. His Phoenix brewery had stables for sixteen horses, along with tackle rooms and feed stores.

Mr Alfred Randall who, from 1949 until his retirement in 1978, worked as a dray driver and groom to J. W. Green's team of dray horses recalls that during the 1950s, the company kept thirteen horses for use on the local rounds and for taking part in competitions and processions. These horses, a mixture of geldings and mares, were impeccably cared for but were expected to work hard for their keep. There were three deliveries each day, Monday to Friday, two in the morning and one in the afternoon. For a barrel delivery two horses were required but only one for a bottle load. Green's at this time had four double drays and four single with two men required for a barrel delivery. The horses were given five meals per day and contrary to popular belief were never given a nose bag of meal during the round.

The stable eventually moved to Latimer Road and Mr Randall recalls that at weekends, not normally working days for the horses, he had to go to the stables and tend his charges. Having spent his life around horses, in the cavalry and yeomanry during the last war, he found life with the dray horses a labour of love and not a burden. The working life of a typical dray horse was twenty years, this after the horses were purchased at around five years old.

Alfred Randall with 'Major', one of J. W. Green's dray horses. (courtesy: Alfred Randall)

During the 1950s, J. W. Green's first grandson, Major John Tabor, was in charge of the spirits division. He lived at Harlington Manor until his death around 1968 and was highly respected by the workforce and liked to be treated as one of 'the lads'.

John William Green became a very wealthy man and resided at The Larches, an elegant villa on the New Bedford Road. The house has since been demolished and the site redeveloped to provide private flats.

Throughout his life Mr Green took the greatest pride in the quality of his beer and the equipment of the premises in which it was brewed. He erected buildings and plant which were unrivalled for their purpose throughout the country. The fame of the Luton brewery under the direction of Green spread far afield, and in due course he acquired the Harpenden Brewery of Messrs. Glover, also the Ampthill Brewery of Messrs. Morris and the Hitchin Brewery of Messrs. Lucas. Thus, before his death in 1932, Green had built up in Luton, a large brewing concern wherein was situated the brewing industries of Luton, Harpenden, Ampthill and Hitchin.

John William Green died on 1st November 1932 and was buried in the Church Cemetery on Crawley Green Road where his headstone is among the grandest in the cemetery. Also interred with him is his wife, Mary Ann, who had passed away nine years earlier, two of his infant children, William and Cyril, who had died aged three and one respectively, in 1876 and 1880. His surviving children Sidney Joseph, Elsie Margaret and Winifred Mabel also lie with their parents. Winifred

The tomb of J. W. Green in the Church cemetery.

had been born on 14th May 1881, and died aged one hundred years and one month on 24th June 1981. Commemorated on the tombstone is his son, Lieutenant Reginald Cumberland Green who was killed in action on 18th May 1916, while serving with the First battalion, Bedfordshire Regiment, on the Western Front. He lies buries in the British Military Cemetery at Arras, France.

John William Green at The Larches about 1930.
(courtesy: Luton Museum and Art Gallery)

In 1954 J. W. Green's merged with Flowers brewery and although Green's was the major part of the merger, the more widely known name of Flowers was retained as the marketing banner. In 1953 Flowers had been the first brewery in Britain to brew and market a keg beer, a product that most of the major breweries were to copy during the next decade.

The old Phoenix Brewery, Park Street West, shortly before demolition.

A typical window of the type to be found in most J. W. Green public houses. This example is to be found at The Engine in Bute Street.

During 1958, Flowers decided that some of the old buildings that had been in constant service for almost a hundred years were in need of replacement. They spent £175,000 to build a new Fermentation and Maturation plant as well as a new Brewhouse. They were faced with the complicated task of constructing the new buildings on premises which some people already regarded as cramped, without hindering production. As space was at a premium, it was decided to build upwards and the new 94ft. high plant was to become a familiar landmark to Lutonians. With the opening of the new buildings the production capacity of the Luton Brewery had been increased by fifty per cent.

In 1962 the London brewers Whitbread (London) Ltd. bought out Flowers and to this day remain the dominant owner and suppliers to the public houses of Luton. The chairman of Flowers at the time of the takeover was Sir Fordham Flower, a direct descendant of Timothy Flower who had been brewing in Hertford over two hundred years before the proposed Whitbread acquisition.

The name of Whitbread, although a comparatively new name to Luton's brewing history, has a long association with Bedfordshire. As long ago as 1254 there were Whitbreads in the north of the county. By 1615 William Whitbread of Gravenhurst was described as a gentleman. The family moved to Cardington, where on 20th August 1720, Samuel Whitbread was born in a comfortable family house called The Barns.

The family fortunes had survived the Civil War, when Whitbread's grandfather had fought for Oliver Cromwell, and as a second-generation Receiver-General for Taxes for the county of Bedfordshire, his father Henry was comfortably off. Samuel was, however, the seventh of eight surviving children – five from a previous marriage. When his father died, Samuel was only seven years old, and his prospects were modest. He was educated for two years by a Northamptonshire clergyman, and at the age of fourteen was sent to London to stay with his step-brother Ive Whitbread.

Within two years, the family paid John Wightman, Master of the Brewers' Company, to take him on as an apprentice in his brewery in Clerkenwell. He left Wightman's Gilport Street Brewery seven months before the end of his seven year apprenticeship, and went into partnership with Godfrey and Thomas Shewell in 1742. (This is the date that appears on all of the Whitbread signs on their public houses.) The value of the partnership was put at £14,116 and comprised two small breweries; the larger, the Goat Brewhouse, on the corner of Old Street and Upper Whitecross Street, and the smaller on the other side of Old Street in Brick Lane, now renamed Central Street. Each brewery had a tap house for retail sales and the firm also owned the leases of fourteen local public houses.

Samuel became the chief brewer at the Goat Brewhouse, but actually brewing beer was only a small part of the business. To begin with, the raw materials had to be acquired and Samuel was hiring his own maltings at Hitchin as early as 1748. He purchased his hops from a factor in Southwark.

Horses were a major expense for a brewery. Whitbread's annual bills to smiths, farriers, wheelwrights and collarmakers, in 1749, were £200, with as much again for hay, straw, oats, beans and bran. The drayhorses themselves cost about £16 each and had a working life of up to fifteen years. The poor mill horses were seldom worth more than £5.

In the first year under Whitbread's management, total production was 18,000 barrels, with the Goat Brewhouse making porter and 'small beer' and the Brick Lane Brewhouse, pale and amber beers.

Whitbread saw the potential for expansion and tried to interest his two partners in the venture. Godfrey Shewell demurred, pulled out his capital and joined another brewer. Samuel and Thomas borrowed money and purchased the derelict King's Head Brewhouse along with a row of adjoining tenements along the south side of Chiswell Street. By 1750, they had demolished the whole site and built a new brewery specifically designed for the production of porter.

Porter was a strong, black beer whose chief advantage seemed to be that it could be made from relatively cheap, coarse barley and robust, less refined hops. It was also ideal for London's soft water. Slightly scorched malt gave it a powerful, nourishing taste as well as its dark colouring. At first, however, its impurities made the beer cloudy and it appealed mainly to heavy manual workers such as food-market porters, who liked its body as much as the fact that it was cheap.

By 1758, production at Chiswell Street was nearly 65,000 barrels, and Whitbread and Shewell had overtaken the Calvert Brothers and Ben Truman to become the largest firm of porter brewers in London.

Shewell retired in 1762, and Whitbread arranged to buy him out for £30,000, payable in instalments between 1765 and 1770. He felt confident to borrow £4,450 and purchased a small estate at Cardington. He later wrote in his property book 'I bought at Cardington because it was the place of my birth and an inheritance of my father, and as it has pleased God to bless me with great abundance'. Over the next twenty-seven years, he spent £60,000 on building up the estate. He also purchased estates in Hertfordshire and at Southill in Bedfordshire. By the time he had finished, his estates were worth in the region of £400,000, equal to about £8 million at today's values.

The Chiswell Street Brewery was in need of expansion, and the inspiration for this came in 1773, when a serious fire destroyed the old porter tun room. The fire was extinguished by £500 worth of beer which burst out of one of the vats. A new storehouse, with enlarged vaults beneath, was built, followed by improvements to the tap house, stables, counting house and the paving of the Great Yard.

Samuel died in 1796, to be succeeded by his son, Samuel, who ran the brewery in conjunction with the senior clerks. It is well that the clerks were able and trustworthy, for Samuel the second did not have much interest or ability to run the business in the same way as his father had. Within weeks of his father's death, the brewery was faced with a cash crisis. The faithful clerks put their own money into the business, and Samuel raised £51,000 from mortgages and loans from his own friends. This enabled the brewery to maintain production for the next three years, before more cash problems forced him into taking his cousin, Jacob Whitbread, Timothy Brown and two of the clerks as partners in the firm. Whitbread and Brown never saw eye to eye and carried on a running feud until at last Brown was paid off in 1810.

Two years later, Whitbread merged with the Martineau Brewery of Lambeth, and the merger came none too soon, for Samuel was beginning to suffer with ill health. His political career was on the wane and he suffered from fatigue and headaches. In 1815, feeling depressed and thinking he was loathed by everybody, he cut his throat with a razor.

Samuel's suicide had left John Martineau facing financial disaster. When Samuel's eldest son, William, joined as a partner in 1816, the business slowly began to recover, but there were still to be some trying years ahead.

In 1834, John Martineau, now seventy-five years old and himself suffering from headaches and fits, took a tasting pipe and began his regular Friday afternoon inspection of the vats. Some time later, one of the overseers went into the vat room and climbed the ladder he found placed against one of them. He found Martineau inside, face down in two feet of beer. At the inquest next day, the medical opinion was that the deceased had been suddenly seized with apoplexy and had fallen into the vat, and the jury returned the verdict: 'Died by the visitation of God'.

The following sixty years saw Whitbread expand into the bottled beer trade with their own branded beer, being one of the pioneers in this new product. They purchased the Anchor Brewery of Lewisham so that they could use the premises as a branch bottling depot to serve the whole of their London market south of the Thames. Five years later they purchased the Bell Brewery at Tottenham for £138,000. Once again the premises were converted into a bottling plant, and the Bells tied houses were supplied from Chiswell Street. This purchase was followed by that of Mathew's and Canning Brewery in Chelsea.

By mid 1900, production was up to nearly 700,000 barrels and profits had climbed to £205,000.

The aftermath of the Great War found the company in a weakened state; they were particularly short of expert management, so they

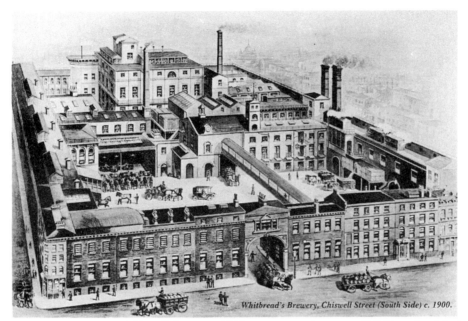

Whitbread's Brewery, Chiswell Street, c. 1900.   *(courtesy: Whitbread archive)*

appointed Sydney Nevile as Managing Director. One of his first tasks was to purchase a 440-acre hop farm in Kent, and eighty per cent of the ordinary shares of a wines and spirits merchant called Stowell and Sons for £20,000.

In 1923, they acquired the Forest Hill Brewery in south London, and with it came the bottled beer marketed as Forest Brown. Whitbread continued brewing this brand and were to have much success with it.

On 29th December 1940, the brewery at Chiswell Street was hit by hundreds of incendiary bombs, and although the hop store, cooperage, stables and malt tower were severely damaged, the brewery was almost undamaged, and was back in production within four days. The same cannot be said for Whitbread's London pubs. A total of 555 public houses, over ninety per cent of their holdings, were damaged in the blitz, with twenty-nine completely destroyed and another forty-nine so battered that they had to close.

The post war Chairman was Colonel Bill Whitbread, a natural leader who had a reputation as a fireball. He found that, although production was at near record levels, the plant and transport were on their last legs, and the pubs Whitbread supplied were battered and worn. The only solution was massive and immediate investment. Bill Whitbread bluntly informed the shareholders that they had two choices. One was to agree to Whitbread becoming a public company, the second was to see it sold or run down. Bill got his way and the company went public. The money raised was used to put Whitbread on a more even keel. The development boom did not get fully into its stride until building restrictions were removed in 1954.

Astute entrepreneurs like Charles Clore and Maxwell Joseph had grasped the potential value of property assets owned by many old-established businesses. Breweries were especially ripe with their strings of public houses, many on High Street sites, and their large brewery premises, once on the edge of town, but now, due to the spread of cities, often all but in the centre. Clore made several approaches for Whitbread, but Colonel Bill was not interested, to the extent of being 'out' when the developer called.

Other family breweries were not so determined and a number in London and the provinces were snapped up by acquisitive companies aware of their dormant asset values. Breweries in smaller towns, however, offered slimmer pickings to the property developers and had time to prepare their defences. Many turned to Whitbread for help to act as a 'white knight' by taking minority shareholdings. Flowers of Luton was one such company.

In 1961, Whitbread acquired the Sheffield brewery of Tennant Bros. and with this purchase came Tennant's Gold Label barley wine, first brewed in 1951 and soon in the Guinness Book of Records as the strongest regularly brewed nationally distributed beer. One year later, they acquired the Luton brewery of Flowers.

At about this time, Bill Whitbread approached Heineken after failing in his attempt to acquire the Belgian Artois Brewery. After long negotiations, a merger took place which resulted in Heineken being brewed under licence at Luton. Heineken insisted that a Dutch brewer must be on site to oversee and ensure that quality control was maintained.

To take advantage of favourable rates of excise duty, a special lower gravity lager was brewed. Heineken originally had doubts, as their product brewed elsewhere was of a stronger brew. Whitbread convinced them that sales of the lower gravity lager would be greater, and this claim was substantiated, with Heineken taking twenty per cent of the UK lager market within two years. Whitbread continued to import some of the higher gravity Heineken as their premium lager, but after coming to a belated agreement with Artois, they restricted the importing of Heineken and instead decided to sell Stella Artois as their flagship lager. In due course, this became the leading high gravity lager in the UK. Stella Artois, like Heineken, is now brewed under licence by Whitbread.

Whitbread's businesses are now managed by four divisions. In March 1990, all of Whitbread's beer production, sales and distribution was integrated into a single business called the Whitbread Beer Company. The previous year, Whitbread Pub Partnerships had been formed to run

The range of bottled beers produced by Flowers Brewery during the 1950s.

the 2,300 tenanted pubs. Whitbread Inns remains responsible for the group's 1,600 managed public houses, which in 1993, sold two million pints of beer and lager. Whitbread Restaurants runs the restaurant businesses, which includes Beefeater Restaurants, Thresher, Pizza Hut, T. G. I. Friday's, Travel Inn and Country Club Hotels. Pizza Hut is a fifty-fifty joint venture with PepsiCo Inc., and the Covent Garden T. G I. Friday's is the busiest Friday's restaurant in the world, in terms of sales.

After the takeover of Flowers Breweries, Whitbread continued to brew at the Park Street West site until 1969 when a new brewery, the first all new brewery to be opened in Britain for over fifty years, opened in Oakley Road. The old brewery site remained standing until 1977 when, after having planning permission to develop the site refused by the council, it was finally demolished. Whitbread has redeveloped the site, along with Capability Green, to include administration and central offices for the whole of the company. To assist the company into further research in brewing products a model brewery is incorporated into the Park Street site.

The new brewery in Oakley Road was the most advanced brewery in Europe, being totally automated under the direction of the master brewer. Gone were the miles of copper piping, open mash tuns, coppers and magnificent shire horses to be replaced by a space age control room with its hundreds of dials and control knobs, a maturation hall containing fifty-nine stainless steel tanks, a £2 million bottling plant and a large fleet of 15-ton articulated delivery trucks.

The bottling plant was the most technologically advanced organisation of its kind in Europe. Rationalisation of design and layout had swept away the drudgery bottling once entailed. A century ago, for instance, a good man would bottle 3,000 bottles a day with the so called 'boot and flogger' method. The Whitbread bottling machines each handled 36,000 bottles an hour and operated sixteen hours each day. By 1976, most of Whitbread's beer was being produced at Luton and at Salmesbury, where a second new brewery had been completed four years earlier. The modernisation programme had not applied to Chiswell Street, where brewing had finally ceased in 1976 after two and a quarter centuries.

For all this investment in technology and quality all was not well in the brewing industry. Some of Whitbread's ventures were looking a little ragged. For the first time labour relations were deteriorating and their repair would take more than a personal plea from the chairman. William Whitbread and the unions had rarely seen eye to eye and labour relations were already fraying before Colonel Bill's retirement. When Whitbread finally faced up to the TGWU at Luton, Robin Farrington, the manager in the firing line, spent almost as much time in the chairman's office reassuring him that they were doing the right thing, as he spent negotiating with the union. Communications with the employees and relations with the unions at Luton continued to decline and as a result the brewery was closed in the middle of 1984 with the loss of 275 jobs. This closure meant, in effect, that for the first time in five hundred years, beer, in any quantity, was no longer brewed in Luton.

The Malting and Brewhouse of William Adams, built 1796. It stood adjacent to the Phoenix Brewery of J. W. Green.

Breweries Located Outside Luton

ADEY and WHITE of St. ALBANS

Stephen Adey and Samuel Monkton White purchased Kinder's brewery in Chequer Street in 1868. Later they bought Parson's Brewery and continued to brew on both sites, producing eleven draught beers, until a serious fire in 1902. White had run the county fire brigade and when fires broke out in St. Albans the shire horses from Chequer Street would be called out to draw the appliances. White died in 1897, with Adey dying two years later.

The company was then run by Harold Adey, son of Stephen. By the end of the First World War he was still only forty-three years of age employing thirty people and owning sixty public houses. He had just acquired the only other brewery left in St. Albans, T. W. Kent and Son, which he subsequently closed taking Reginald Kent into partnership.

In 1921 Adey and White became a limited company, building new offices in Victoria Road. May 1936 saw them accept an offer for their brewery and fifty-six public houses from J. W. Green. Two months later the brewery was closed with the site being sold to St. Albans Corporation.

BANKS and TAYLOR

Founded in 1981, in a small industrial unit in Shefford, by Martin Leigh Ayres and Michael Andre Desquesnes. Martin Ayres had previously worked for Whitbread in their property office. They appointed as their master brewer John Waters, and concentrated on making real ale, which is well regarded by connoisseurs. They were voted best new brewery beer by CAMRA in 1988. The brewery at one time owned nine tied houses, three of them in Luton and its free trade in London and the Home Counties reached some 250 outlets.

The range of beers produced included Shefford Bitter, Shefford Mild, Shefford Pale Ale, Dragon Slayer, Shefford Old Strong, Shefford Old Dark, Edwin Taylor's Extra Stout (named after Martin Taylor's great grandfather), 2XS, Black Bat and Old Bat. The last two were mainly seasonal ales due to the high specific gravity.

In April 1994, after cash flow problems, the Official Receiver was called in and took over the running of the company. Seven of the leases of the original pubs were given up under the Receiver and of the ten employees, six were released. The two partners, plus one other person, were successful in buying the rights to the brewing side of the business and it is now operated under the name of B and T Brewery Ltd. The full range of beers continues to be produced and there is great optimism as to the future of the company.

BASS CHARRINGTON

In 1777, William Bass, the owner of a carrying business in Burton upon Trent, purchased the Bass Town House, together with a plot of land complete with tun house and malt house, and established his first brewery.

Burton upon Trent was already famous as a brewing town when William Bass arrived. The monks of Burton Abbey, founded in 1002, had discovered that the special quality of Burton well water was well suited to the production of fine beers. Having built a reputation for quality beers, based on the best water, barley and hops, he left a thriving business to his son Michael Thomas Bass when he died in 1787.

Michael developed the export side of the business to such an extent that Bass had an unparalleled reputation in Eastern Europe and Russia. The Napoleonic wars brought an end to the Baltic trade and business languished, resulting in many Burton brewers failing. Bass looked around for new opportunities and their sights fell on India where there was a need for a light, sparkling beer. The result of their toils was India Pale Ale, later abbreviated to IPA, which was an instant success and exported in thousands of barrels and bottles through the ports of Liverpool and Hull.

In 1827, Michael died, leaving the brewing business to his son, Michael Thomas the second. This Michael became the great entrepreneur of nineteenth century brewing, turning the company into the greatest in the world before his death in 1884.

When William Bass first began to brew in Burton, his output was a few hundred barrels each year. By 1797, this had increased to 2,000 barrels, and by 1831, to 10,000 barrels. The coming of the railways in 1839, and the growing fame of Bass beers saw production increase in leaps and bounds, so that by the Bass Centenary in 1877, the output was nearing 1,000,000 barrels, annually.

Bass beers were to be found the world over and the painter, Manet, immortalised two bottles of Bass in his famous painting 'The bar at the Folies Bergère'. In America, Bass beers were listed on the menu of the dining cars of the Union Pacific transcontinental railroad.

The label incorporating the famous Bass Red Triangle is the world's oldest registered trade mark. With the introduction of the Trade Marks Registration Act of 1875, a loyal member of the Bass staff spent an uncomfortable night on the steps of the registrar's office to ensure first entry to the office the following morning so that the triangle, which the company had used since 1855, would hold the coveted No. 1 place. Bass continued to grow throughout this century and in 1962 they merged with Mitchells and Butlers, followed in 1967 by a merger with Charrington United Breweries to form Bass Charrington.

The story of Charrington, one of the great London brewers, goes back to the eighteenth century. John Charrington was born in 1739 in Aldenham, Hertfordshire, the son of the local rector. As a young man he was apprenticed to a brewery in Islington where he proved ideally suited to the brewing business and in 1766, he bought a one-third share in the firm of Wastfield and Moss, who had brewed at the Anchor Brewery in Mile End since 1743. Wastfield retired in 1768, and John Charrington bought his share. Moss retired fifteen years later and John Charrington and his brother Harry then had control of a thriving business. They prospered, and by 1800, Charrington and Co. were second in the list of London's ale breweries with 15,556 barrels of ale produced in the year.

John died, aged seventy-six, in 1815 and his son Nicholas, took over, but in 1827, he too had died and the company passed to his sons, Edward and Spencer. They developed the business by acquiring other breweries and by increasing the range of their brewing activities.

When John Charrington established his business, the Anchor Brewery stood in open fields, but as the brewery expanded and developed, so did the surrounding areas, providing new customers for Charrington ales. Most years there appeared new buildings, equipment and machinery at the Mile End site.

By the end of the nineteenth century, Charrington was one of London's largest and most successful brewers and a programme of acquisition was instituted. This policy was continued into this century with no fewer than forty-nine breweries becoming part of the Charrington organisation between 1833 and the early 1950s. The most significant acquisition was that of Hoare and Co. in 1933. Although the company was founded in 1700, the Red Lion Brewery actually dated back to 1492 and they had significant business through their pub estate. The links with the Hoare brewery also resulted in their trademark – the Toby jug – being adopted for Charrington houses and beers. In 1962, Charrington merged with United Brewers in the North of England to form Charrington United Breweries. Five years later came the merger with Bass Mitchells and Butlers.

In the middle of the last century, it was commonplace for innkeepers to brew the beer they offered for sale. This was certainly true of Mr Henry Mitchell, licensee of the Oddfellows Arms beerhouse in Hall Street, West Bromwich. He was born at Bromyard in Worcestershire in 1810 and by 1851, was in the licenced trade as landlord of the Oddfellows Arms. One year later he decided to move to a larger house, also with brewing

A modern Bass delivery truck. This brewery tractor unit was designed by AWD Trucks of Dunstable in 1991 to specifications laid down by Bass Charrington and featured air suspension.

facilities and chose the Cape Hill Brewery between West Bromwich and Smethwick. After another move in 1854, to the Crown Inn, Oldbury Road, Smethwick, he was joined by his son, Henry the second, who was to build the Cape Hill Brewery.

William Butler was born at Hinckley in Leicestershire in 1843. At age sixteen he was working behind the bar at the Old Crown Inn, Broad Street, which at that time was a very impressive establishment. In 1866 William went into the licenced trade on his own by taking possession of the London Works Tavern in Smethwick. He expanded the business, gaining a high reputation for his beer, so much so that in 1875 he entered into a partnership with his previous boss at the Old Crown Inn.

Meanwhile, Henry Mitchell the second, wanting to break away from the business of home-brewing, built a new brewery on land adjoining the Crown Inn and set about increasing the trade. Fourteen brews each week were brewed out of one mash tun and he had small maltings in use in West Bromwich, Smethwick and Birmingham. Space was at a premium, so in 1878 he purchased land between the Birmingham boundary and Smethwick for the site of his new brewery. The first brick for the Crown Brewery was laid on March 21st 1878, with the first brew being produced in July of the following year.

Later, when Mitchell and Butler were looking for further expansion for their respective breweries, their mutual respect for each other made it a natural move for them to join together in partnership. All brewing operations were concentrated at the Crown Brewery and the new company of Mitchells and Butlers prospered. By 1900 the site had grown to over sixty acres and employed 1,000 people. They had a policy of providing clean, airy public houses with more than a passing thought for customers' well being. 'Good Honest Beer' became the company's watchword. In 1962 they merged with Bass and in 1967, when Charrington joined forces they became part of the Bass Charrington empire.

BENNETT'S

Benjamin Bennett ran a small but successful brewery business in Dunstable, but by 1874 he was also leasing what had been Healey's Brewery in High Street Harpenden, otherwise known as Curtis's Brewery. In 1882 he leased the Redbourn Brewery for a term of eighteen years. By 1893 he was described as Bennett of Harpenden when he acquired the White Horse, High Barnet to add to the two he already owned in St. Albans. In 1897, by the direction of the Hon. F Bowes Lyon, the Redbourn Brewery estate and its nine pubs were auctioned. There was no buyer for the brewery but the public houses were bought by other local brewers, including Thomas Sworder.

Bennett died in 1906 but his Dunstable brewery continued in business until 1938 when it was taken over, with fifty-nine public houses, by Mann, Crossman and Paulin. The buildings were finally demolished in 1971.

BENSKINS

Joseph Benskin arrived in Watford during 1867 and purchased, at auction, the Cannon Brewery which had been founded by John Dyson over one hundred years earlier. Joseph was a retired hotel owner and what convinced him to pay £34,000 and re-enter working life remains a mystery. The 1871 census describes him as a common brewer employing sixteen men, two boys, a cook and a housemaid.

Upon his death, his son John, his son-in-law and master brewer Walter Green ran the brewery then known as Benskins and Co. Due to ill health, John retired and his younger brother Thomas took over and went into partnership with James Panton. Business trebled in four years, probably due to James Panton who was quoted as to being the first brewer to study scientific brewing at London University.

Output rose to 45,000 gallons a week and fifty hogsheads (fifty-four gallons each) a week of IPA were prepared to export to India. A railway siding of the LNWR was built right into the brewery premises, with a full train load leaving every day. During the Great War the nearby Cassio Wharf, on the Grand Union canal, was used to ship cargos of produce to London Docks and thereby to the Continent.

The business became a private limited company in 1894 known as Benskins Watford Brewery Ltd. Between 1897 and 1898 the company purchased many smaller breweries and became the largest brewers in Hertfordshire. About this time, the Pennant sign was adopted as the company logo, apparently at the suggestion of one of the Benskin daughters, and the Cannon name was thereafter only used as the address of the brewery.

There now followed a period of consolidation as Benskins moved into the 20th century. Expansion began again in 1913 with purchases of breweries in Berkhamsted, Bishop Stortford, Aston Clinton and Saffron Walden, the last being purchased from Watney Combe Reid and Co. In 1927 they took over control of Roberts and Wilson Ltd. of Ivinghoe.

After another buy-out in 1951 a local paper reported the amazing fact that in nine years 463 breweries had been merged into larger concerns. The concept that 'bigger is best' was debated for many years and in 1957 Benskins finally accepted a bid from Ind Coope which resulted in the business and 636 houses changing hands. Ind Coope continued to expand and were re-formed in 1963, along with Tetley Walkers and Ansells, as Allied Breweries. Brewing continued on the site until 1972 when Watford Borough Council bought it. The brewery was eventually demolished in 1978, the office buildings remaining and being converted into Watford Museum.

Benskins bitter is now brewed in Burton but its links with Watford are still strong. A special commemorative ale was brewed in 1984 to celebrate Watford football club reaching the FA Cup Final.

COURAGE

John Courage was the son of an exiled French Huguenot family who had settled in Aberdeen. He left Scotland and moved to London where he prospered in the flourishing maritime trade on the River Thames, acting as an agent for the Carron ships which plied from Glasgow Wharf on the north bank.

In 1787 he decided to diversify his interests by going into brewing, on a site he had noticed by the Southwark foreshore. He purchased a brewhouse at Horselydown for the sum of £616. 13s. 11d, and paid by cheque on December 20th. Within the year the first entry in the brewing book stated that 'John Courage from Aberdeen had brewed fifty-one barrels of beer in his brewery'. He lived only ten years after this first entry, but during this time his priorities had changed. He became first a brewer and second a shipping man. He left a widow, Harriot, three daughters and a three year old son, John. As they had lived on the brewery premises, his wife was sufficiently familiar with the day to day management to run the affairs of Horselydown with the help of managing clerk John Donaldson, until such a time as her son should be ready to take over. Unfortunately, she died in 1797, so John Donaldson took over as a partner and charged with the care of the young children. In 1800 the firm was described as Courage and Donaldson Brewers and carried that title until 1851.

Young John entered the brewery at age twenty-one in 1811, the business prospering under the partnership and by Donaldson's retirement in 1836, around fifty years after the founding, the business had increased two hundredfold and the buildings at the brewery had multiplied. Two of Donaldson's sons joined the brewery, but in 1851 Courage bought out their shares and became sole owner.

He purchased various wharves on the river frontage, an astute move as they provided access for the incoming malt, coal, timber and forage for the horses and the outgoing beers and stouts, bound for Lowestoft, Dundee and Leith. In fact the river played such an important role that the firm ran its own lightermen and barges.

John consolidated the business and also the dynasty which bears his name. One year after the Donaldson's partnership had been dissolved, he took into partnership his two older sons, John and Robert. Thus, in 1852, the business became wholly a family concern. Two years later, John the second died and John the third began a brief reign with his brothers Robert and Edward as partners. After his death, another brother, Henry, was admitted into the firm.

Courage began to establish working arrangements with other brewing concerns, especially as it was realised that the water from the Horselydown well, although fine for the production of traditional London beers such as mild ale and stout, lacked the mineral ingredients required for a good bitter ale. They recognised the need to supply their customers with this product, so in 1872 they contracted with Flower and Son of Stratford-on-Avon, brewers of a fine beer, to supply them with bitter for their own distribution.

In April 1888, the Courage family partnership, having existed for just over a century, came to an end with the formation of the limited company Courage and Co. At this time, the brewery's transport arrangements were a matter of pride. There were seventy-nine dray horses, purchased in the main from North Wales and Cheshire at an average of £80 each. They were, in general sixteen and a half hands high and would each draw two tons. There were thirty-five drays on the firm, twenty large and fifteen small. The former were three horse drays loading up to twenty-five barrels and the latter fifteen barrels. The brewery

The Courage Brewery at Horselydown Lane, 1947. (courtesy: Courage Group)

employed two hundred men and had an output of over 300,000 barrels.

During May 1891 there was an explosion in the malt mills which set light to the brewhouse. The resultant fire burned for several days, defeating the efforts of the land and river fire services, with the total loss of the brewhouse. The resilience of the company then came to the fore with an arrangement with Messrs. Barclay and Perkins to supply all the London beers required by Courage to fulfil their commitments. This arrangement lasted for about one month until brewing started again at Horselydown. The friendship forged between these two brewing concerns would result in a merger some sixty-four years later.

move outside of London in the creation of the structure which was to become the Courage Group. This was in 1903 and was initially purchased so that Courage could brew their own pale ales and bitter and not have to rely on Flower and Son.

The first mechanical vehicle purchased by Courage was a steam Foden, bought in 1916 for £673. Between the wars the Foden steamers were a popular form of brewery transport which are still nostalgically remembered by older people and, when they can be found, collected by veteran enthusiasts. Courage purchased their first Commer car during the First World War and in 1920, their first K type Leyland motor lorry. By 1930 they were running thirty-four Leyland's, five Foden's, five Morris trucks and three trailers. They also retained a stud of thirty-two horses.

The acquisition of freehold interest at Horselydown gave the company a free hand to carry out a rebuilding policy which started in 1925. A steam cooperage, which had been instituted after the fire of 1891, was reinstalled and by 1932 the company was making all its own casks from its own timber. By the 1960s not a single cask was being made at Horselydown, or indeed throughout the many breweries in the Courage Group. Steel had taken over.

With the takeover of the Camden Brewery and the Farnham United Breweries Company on the Surrey–Hampshire border, the Courage group was established as a metropolitan concern with breweries north and south of the Thames. Between 1930 and 1943 Courage acquired the ownership of Noakes Brewery of Bermondsey, the Kidd Brewery at Dartford and Hodgson's Kingston Brewery.

The brewhouse was badly damaged by enemy bombing during the war which resulted in a new brewhouse built and opened in 1954. One year later, Courage joined forces with Barclay Perkins of the famous Anchor Brewery, just up the river above London Bridge.

The Anchor Brewery, built on the site of Shakespeare's Globe Theatre, had been an established feature of Southwark for several centuries, under various names and owners, before David Barclay and John Perkins acquired possession in 1781. The previous owner, Henry Thrale, had died one month before and the business had been put onto the market. By 1810, two hundred men were employed and there was stabling for a hundred horses. The stock of liquor was valued at £300,000.

A serious fire almost destroyed the site in 1832 but resulted in benefits for the brewery as it enabled a fine Victorian institute to be built, replacing many antiquated buildings. During the early years of this century, Barclay Perkins, like many others, went through a lean period, but fortunes began to build after the war, and in 1929 they took over Style and Winch Ltd., the Dartford Brewery Co. and the Royal Brewery, Brentford Ltd.

A major overseas enterprise of the fifties was the establishment of the Blue Nile Brewery at Khartoum in the Republic of Sudan. This was the first brewery to be started in that country and the first to be planned and built overseas by any of the companies destined to form the Courage Group. This new brewery coincided with the merger of Courage and Barclay Perkins.

The Barclay Perkins brewhouse at Southwark in the mid-nineteenth century.
(courtesy: Courage Group)

In 1960, Simonds Brewery of Reading joined the Courage group and brought with them 1,200 tied houses, hotels and catering establishments, as well as a chain of retail wine and spirit shops operating under the name of Arthur Cooper Ltd.

One year later, Georges Brewery of Bristol merged with the Group and made sure that the west of England was well covered for the parent firm.

John Smith's Tadcaster Brewery, with 1,800 pubs, hotels and freehold clubs, spread over Yorkshire, Lancashire, Derbyshire, County Durham, Cheshire, Lincolnshire, Nottinghamshire and parts of Cambridgeshire and Shropshire merged with Courage in 1970. During the 1960s, the Group was employing 15,000 people and producing 75 million gallons of beer per annum.

In March 1991, the Courage Group gained control of Watney Mann from Grand Metropolitan Breweries. This arrangement, which is to be reviewed in 1996, meant that Courage Group run the brewing side of the business and Grand Metropolitan run the licenced houses. Courage Group breweries are situated in Reading, Bristol, Tadcaster and Halifax.

FLOWER of HERTFORD

Timothy Flower ran the Turks Head coffee house at 42 Fore Street in 1725, with a brewhouse in the yard, and he was followed by Mary Flower. Richard Flower and John Fordham leased the brewery in Brewery Lane from Timothy Ireland in 1785 becoming legal partners in November of that year. The company was dissolved in 1792 when Flower paid £2,025 for Fordham's half share. Flower sold his half share back to Fordham provided Flower could lease it for thirty-one years.

Flower left the brewery business in 1803, selling his interest to two Baldock maltsters, George and Thomas Wells Fitzjohn. The Flower family emigrated to America in 1818, but Richard's youngest son, Edward Fordham Flower, returned in 1824 re-entering the brewery business in a brewery near Shaftesbury, Dorset. This later transferred to Stratford-on-Avon, where it became a household name, merging with J. W. Green in 1954 until its take-over by Whitbread in 1961.

FORDHAM of ASHWELL

In 1796 the Fordhams took over the lease of the land from Whitbread. The founder was Elias Pym Fordham, a woolstapler, banker and brewer. New buildings were erected in 1825 and 1839.

E. P. Fordham is said to have knocked over a drunken man in an accident and the man blamed Fordham's Ale. He sold off his holding to his son Oswald for £100 in 1833. Oswald ran the brewery, until his death in 1862, with his elder brother Edward, who died in 1889. The company became E. K. and H. Fordham in 1864 when the surviving brother amalgamated with his cousin Herbert Fordham of Odsey Grange.

Sir Herbert Fordham managed the brewery until his death in 1929. Then William Herbert Fordham returned from his job as a mining engineer in Europe to run the business for thirty-five years. Under him the brewery was acquired, in 1952, by J. W. Green. The Ashwell brewery became a bottle store, all production being based at Luton. It closed in 1965, the site being redeveloped into modern housing in 1969.

GLOVER and SONS of HARPENDEN

In 1898 Richard Glover of the Wenlock Brewery, London, purchased the Peacock Brewery for £58,000 from the trustees of the old James Mardall. He demolished the buildings and rebuilt the site, including the tower, which was later used by the Waverley Mills. In 1902 Glover, and his forty public houses, amalgamated with Pryor, Reid and Company to form the Hatfield and Harpenden Brewery Company Ltd. with

£163,000 capital, but continued to brew under their own name. By 1910 they were listed as Glover and Sons Ltd. 1919 saw the company go into liquidation, with J. W. Green buying the brewery and some of the pubs, others being sold to various brewers later in the year. The buildings were used by a hosiery firm and known as Waverley Mills, until demolition in 1936.

GREENE KING (BIGGLESWADE) LTD

After the merger with Wells and Winch in 1961, activities at Biggleswade continued as before for a short time. Poor sales soon began to improve with the addition to the stocked beers of Abbot Ale, (one of the finest ales brewed, in the opinion of the author), Harvest Brown and Farm Stout.

The annual report for 1962 showed that the first year's trading had been a success. By 1963 two public houses had been rebuilt and one new house completed by the brewery's own builders.

The Company name was changed to Greene King (Biggleswade) Ltd. at the same time as Simpson's Brewery Ltd. became Greene King

A Greene King delivery truck built by Bedford 1980. It stands in front of the Brewhouse and Water Tower.   *(courtesy: Greene King)*

(Baldock) Ltd. The Company came up-to-date by installing new technology in the offices. A new fleet of Bedford trucks was purchased, all of them displaying the Company logo.

The group reorganised in 1965 by closing the Baldock site and using the Bury St. Edmunds base to supply forty ex-Wells and Winch houses in Cambridge and eastwards and using Biggleswade to supply twenty-two ex-Bury houses to the west of Cambridge. Three new pubs were opened in 1967 in Bedford, Hitchin and Luton to replace forty that had been closed since the merger. Trade had increased four years later to 68,000 barrels brewed at Biggleswade and total sales of 81,000 barrels.

Greene King's first cask conditioned beer, King Keg, was introduced in 1962 and Audit Ale followed within the year. A new keg plant was built in 1977 with the capacity to fill 393 kegs an hour rising to 687 kegs an hour with further improvement to the plant. It was responsible for all keg ales and also for lager production since the Company had taken a two per cent holding in Harp Lager.

By 1976, with trade still on the increase, the brews available from Biggleswade were – XX dark mild, KK light mild, IPA bitter, Abbot Ale, King Keg, Keg Abbot plus the newly introduced Yeoman bitter. The holding in Harp Lager went from two to twenty per cent and to twenty-five per cent in 1979, the other seventy-five per cent being owned by Guinness. The decision to concentrate cask beer at Bury St. Edmunds was taken in 1988 and a new Biggleswade brewery to replace the old one was started on 2nd January 1989 with the first brew from it being produced on 14th February 1990.

HEALEY of HARPENDEN

George Healey, of the Watford Brewery, purchased Curtis's Harpenden Brewery in 1853. George was born at Deptford in 1819 and by age forty-two he was a brewer and maltster, employing twelve men and one boy. He died in 1862 and the business was run by his widow Elizabeth. She was aged forty-five in 1871 and by 1874 she was leasing the brewery to Bennett. After her death, in 1893, the brewery was sold, with eighteen public houses, for £6,000 to Mardall's who were brewing nearby.

The Healey brewery in Watford was situated in King Street with the entrance to it in George Street. They purchased premises in the High Street from which to run the wine and spirit side of the business. In 1898, Benskins bought out the brewery side of Healey's along with fifteen public houses and one off-licence. The wine and spirit site had already been sold to Durand, Sedgewick and Bird in 1890.

LATTIMORE of WHEATHAMPSTEAD

The Lattimore family were brewing for most of the nineteenth century at the Hope Brewery. This brewery had been built by James Wilkins of Wheathampstead in 1781. James Wilkins was the brewer who purchased the Wheelplough brewery in Park Street Luton.

The Lattimore family took over the brewery in 1839 and remained on site until 1897 when they severed their connection with the Hope brewery. They leased its tied houses to Pryor Reid and Company, and the brewery with its seven houses was put up for sale in November 1904.

LUCAS BROTHERS of HITCHIN

The Lucas Brewery was established in 1709 and in its early years was run by William Lucas and his brother-in-law Isaac Gray. They took over Conquest's brewery in Hitchin some time after 1727. For six generations the eldest son was named William Lucas and was in charge of the brewery, later with one or more brothers. William Lucas (1768–1846) was in partnership with his brother Joseph, to whom he left active management of the brewery after their father's death in 1819. In 1837 the firm was briefly known as Lucas and Jeeves but normally it was William and Joseph, later with the addition of William junior. The latter's brother Samuel (1805–1870) came into the brewery in 1834. Though Samuel was committed to the brewery he was also an exceptional artist and combined his trips to London to buy barley and hops with visits to fellow artists and studios. In 1865 Samuel suffered a stroke and his son Samuel followed into the business and proceeded to expand with interests in the Barnsley Brewery and elsewhere. He broke with the family's Quaker tradition and became an Anglican. The business became a limited company in 1896, trading as W & S Lucas Ltd. a name that often appears on bottles, as does their trademark of an arm with a dagger.

At this time, the brewery on Sun Street had buildings for the production and storage of beer, a mineral water factory, cooperage, cask and bottle washing departments, carpenters' and engineers' shops. The bottled beer they were producing in 1907 was allowed to mature naturally in the bottle, with no artificial carbonisation.

In 1920 the company seemed to be in good health with over fifty licenced houses in Hertfordshire and Bedfordshire when out of the blue in 1921 it was reported that Messrs. J. W. Green Ltd. of the Luton Brewery had acquired the Hitchin Brewery of Messrs. W. S. Lucas Ltd. It was intended to operate the Hitchin concern entirely separately from the Luton Brewery and it was not proposed to alter the name. However, in 1923 the brewery was closed and the buildings were finally demolished in 1963, by which time Green's had themselves been taken over by Whitbread.

The family's connection with the brewing industry had long been an embarrassment to some members. William Lucas (1804–1861) had written in his diary that his father 'did not wish his sons to come into the brewery, but the property being so much tied up in it, they could not do otherwise than continue the trade which had been in the family for more than a century'.

The Lucas family did a great deal for Hitchin and for their employees. Joseph's daughter Phebe remembered 'suppers for the draymen and workmen in the brewery – substantial meals of roast and boiled beef and mutton with plum pudding for second course', and she also recalled a vast throng of men and women on St. Thomas's day when the firm gave a dole of one penny to any who liked to ask for it.

MARDALL of HARPENDEN

James Mardall purchased the Peacock brewery around 1870. By 1882 it was being run by Mrs Martha Mardall and the trustees of James Mardall. They sold the concern, in 1898, to Richard Glover of London. Previously, in October 1893, Mrs Mardall had acquired her main competitor, Healey's Harpenden Brewery.

McMULLEN and SONS Ltd

Peter McMullen was born in 1799 and by 1825 was, by profession, a master cooper. He operated his business in Back Street, Hertford, selling his casks and barrels to ten small brewing companies that were already established in Hertford Town. In 1827, he decided to go into the brewing business, brewing his beer in his back garden shed. He obviously thrived because within three years he moved to a full-scale commercial brewery, known as the Millbridge Brewery.

He bought his first public house, The Greyhound at Bengeo, in 1836, paying £481 for the pub, four acres of ground and six little cottages. The pub is still standing today although considerably altered from its original days. The price of this first public house venture is cheap compared to one of their latest acquisitions, The Spice of Life, in the centre of Soho, which cost a staggering £3.5 million.

By the time of Peter's retirement in 1860, the Company had become one of the successful Hertfordshire breweries. Two of his sons, Alexander Peter and Osmond Henry, carried on the business as P. McMullen and Sons.

One of the first beers brewed was McMullen Original AK which first saw the light of day around 1832. This highly regarded traditional beer with its unique malty taste is still brewed, 160 years later.

Company expansions in 1864, when they purchased the Cannon Brewery in Ware along with all its pubs, and in 1874, when the Star Brewery of Ware with twenty public houses, eventually meant that the Millbridge Brewery could no longer cope with the extra demand. Therefore, in 1891, McMullen's built an all new brick brewery in Hartham Lane, Hertford, and it became known as The Hertford Brewery. A feature of this new brewery was a 140 foot deep artesian well, so that pure quality water could be drawn to provide the liquor with which to brew their products.

Alexander McMullen retired in 1896, with Osmond Henry carrying on and becoming a limited company in 1898. The public house holding at this time amounted to over ninety premises. 1904 saw the purchase of the Waltham Abbey Brewery and pubs, followed six years later by the Epping Brewery and tied estate.

Shortly after Osmond Henry's golden wedding anniversary in 1913, he died leaving his son, Osmond Robert, to continue the family tradition. He purchased the Baker Hope Brewery of Hertford in 1920, this being the last of the ten breweries that had been supplied with casks by the founder almost a hundred years earlier.

A period of consolidation followed with the business making some secure financial investments. However, with Osmond Robert's death in 1946, and horrendous death duties due, the company was threatened with bankruptcy. The two sons of Osmond Robert, Osmond James and Robert Peter, were determined to see the Company survive, mortgaging half the entire business to the Prudential Assurance Company and demanding a re-assessment of the death duty. It was many years before the Company was able to stabilise itself, the demand for keg beers in the early 1970s being instrumental in providing the confidence to invest one million pounds in the production of McMullen Castle keg, now known as McMullen No. 1 Draught Special Bitter. The increased demand for quality lager throughout the 1970s, saw the building of a new brewery, built behind the existing one, and turned over to brew and launch Hartsman Lager.

The standing of the Company today is stronger than at any time during its history, owning over one hundred and fifty public houses and a chain of off-licences. The business is in the hands of four members of the McMullen family, with eighty-nine per cent of the voting shares owned by twenty-two members of the family. With many young McMullens still to attain working age, no doubt entering the brewery when they do, the future of the only surviving independent Hertfordshire brewery looks bright for the next 160 years.

PARSONS of ST. ALBANS

Though the Parsons family owned public houses in Sandridge in 1765, and St. Albans by 1765, the first to be called a brewer was Henry Parsons in 1832. He had become a freeman of the borough in 1820 and owned the White Swan, which was next door to his brewhouse on St. Peter Street, his maltings being down Holywell Hill.

Henry died in 1870 and was succeeded by his younger son Francis. Upon his death, aged forty-two in 1885, the brewery was sold at auction to Adey and White, but the Parsons family continued to lease them their fourteen pubs.

PRYOR of HATFIELD

The Hatfield brewery of James Spurrell was purchased for £34,000 in 1837 by the Pryor family. Alfred Pryor ran it until his death in 1876 when his son Edward bought it for £29,442. He and his brother-in-law Percy Reid became partners in 1881, purchasing, during the next fifteen years, three other breweries, becoming Pryor Reid and Company Ltd. with 133 tied houses and capital of £95,000. In 1902 they merged with Glovers to form Hatfield and Harpenden Breweries Ltd., though trading continued under separate names.

Edward died in 1904 and Percy lost his only son, Geoffrey, during the Great War. There being no successor, the business closed in March 1920 with Benskins buying all 107 public houses.

REDBOURN BREWERY

In 1866 Thomas and John Edwards were brewing at Redbourn and had just one Luton inn under their ownership. In 1882 they were taken over by Bennett's of Dunstable.

SIMPSON of BALDOCK

The brewery that was built by Robert Thurgood, between 1730 and his death in 1775, on High Street, Baldock was called the Georgian Brewery. After his death the business was left to his daughter Sarah, who was married to a Watford Brewer, Thomas Cluterbuck.

John Pryor purchased the brewery in 1799, after having leased it for a number of years, and in 1819 it passed to his son, John Izzard Pryor. This Quaker family built up their business by acquiring small breweries and public houses in the Baldock area; among these were Fitzjohn's and the

Ind's Brewery. Within ten years John leased the brewery to his sons, Morris and John, after which he moved to Walkern. The sons owned 120 public houses, which was a considerable number for a small rural brewery.

The brothers of John Izzard senior, Thomas and Robert, were themselves brewers, being partners in Truman, Hanbury and Buxton of London. Another brother, Alfred, ran the Hatfield Brewery which later became Pryor, Reid and Co. Ltd.

John, the son, died in 1853 and Morris, not wishing to carry on the business by himself, sold out to two brothers, Thomas and Joseph Simpson, for £80,904. These brothers had connections in the trade as they were nephews of the Royston brewer John Phillips. The firm traded as Simpson and Co. until 1935 when the private company, Simpson's Brewery Ltd. was set up with Miss Evelyn Shaw-Hellier, grand-daughter of Joseph Simpson, as the majority shareholder.

Profits were good and at least one-third of them were put back into improvements and also into a reserve fund. Production had increased from 12,000 barrels annually in 1826 to 25,000 barrels in 1964 with 125 tied houses to be supplied. The company had been steadily buying pubs, but at the same time selling off uneconomical premises, so that the total number controlled hardly increased. In 1926 they purchased twelve premises from Wrights of Walkern who had ceased brewing two years earlier. All of their tied properties were situated within twenty miles of the brewery, nine of them in Luton.

Baldock High Street in 1965, Simpson's Brewery with the brewhouse to the right.
(courtesy: Greene King)

By the late 1940s, profits were running at around £42,000 and some was invested in a new bottling line in 1950.

To avoid huge death duties, Miss Shaw-Hellier was advised to sell the business. Preferring to deal with Greene King, rather than one of the brewing giants, she accepted an offer of £525,000, in 1954, made up partly from cash and partly Greene King shares.

In 1963 the brewery became Greene King (Baldock) Ltd. with brewing coming to an end in 1965, although bottling was continued for some time. The site was then sold to Baldock UDC and most of it was demolished in 1968 to make way for housing development. The Brewery House, Manor House and part of the Engine house were to remain.

STEED BREWERY of BALDOCK

John Steed bought the brewery behind the Star and the old Black Eagle in 1831. He had leased it from William Oliver in 1823 and was buying pubs in 1828. New buildings were erected in 1840 and he continued to brew until at least 1867. When he died in 1877 his son Oliver succeeded him until his death in 1888. His widow, Margaret, sold the brewery in 1889 to William Pickering, when it was called the Pale Ale Brewery.

After a spell under Morley and then the Baldock Brewing Company from 1898, it was acquired in 1904, with twenty-two houses, for £13,000, by Wells and Winch. Activity continued until 1938 and then the site stood empty, with a scrap metal merchant occupying the yard until it was demolished in 1969.

WATNEY

In 1837 James Watney, a miller, purchased a quarter share in the Stag Brewery, in partnership with John Lettsom Elliot and Charles Lambert, for a term of fourteen or twenty-one years as the partners might agree. The Stag Brewery had begun life around 1607, when William Greene occupied the Talbot Inn at the end of Cabidge Lane, now Castle Lane, in the vicinity of what was to become Victoria Station in London.

After his death, members of the family extended the site, and by 1636 John Greene is shown as lessee of the property. Five years later, he was succeeded by his son, William, the first known brewer of the Stag Brewhouse. Under the Greene family the business grew from strength to strength and while the business was prospering, William enlisted in the Kings army, in 1646, during the Civil War, being promoted to major. On the accession of Charles the Second he was dubbed a knight, whereupon he retired to the village of Mitcham in Surrey, leaving the brewery management to his cousin John.

Until the opening of the Chelsea Waterworks, close to the Stag Brewery, the water had been supplied by the York Waterworks, the water from it being described, in 1753, as 'cabbageous, dead-dogitous, dead-catifious, fishstreethillious and Drury-lanious'. Whether the consumers of their beers were aware of the condition of the basic ingredient is not recorded, but they made enough profit to open two more breweries, one in Fulham and the other situated at Kensington gravel pits.

By 1690, a third generation Greene was in charge of the brewery, and with the business of beer production booming it was estimated that the output of the London breweries was 2,000,000 barrels annually.

In 1715 William Greene completely rebuilt the brewery on a scale hitherto unsurpassed by any other brewer in the country. The surveyor's measurements appended to the insurance policy give a clear picture of the different buildings. The largest was the great Brewhouse, 111 feet by 83 feet, with a value of £1,000. Equal in value was the Pale Brew House with its long malt lofts, 110 feet by 40 feet. The Tun Store House was a third large structure, valued at £600, 107 feet by 33 feet. Then there were the Great Stables and the Dray Horse Stable, near which were the Horse Pond and another stable for mill horses. The Cooperage, Coach-house and other outbuildings completed the schedule. It was described in 1722 by William Stow in his 'Remarks on London' as 'the finest brewhouse in Europe'.

The fortunes of the business, however, began to decline under the control of Edward Burnaby Greene, who preferred to concentrate on a literary career, to such an extent, that by 1760 the Stag Brewery was not even listed in the eight leading breweries in London. New names were arising to seize the trade from those who were content to rest on their laurels. Truman, Courage, Whitbread Gyfford, Hucks, Barclay and later Meux, Combe Reid were all vying for the title of London's top brewery. In 1787 the brewery was put into the hands of the receiver, and the lease was taken over by a new firm of brewers trading as Moore, Elliot and Company, later to become Elliot, Watney and Co.

The Watneys first emerged from the past in the neighbourhood of Wimbledon during the early eighteenth century, with the birth, in 1705, of Daniel Watney, the earliest known ancestor of the brewing family. He had four sons, three of them, William, Thomas and John, surviving and becoming farmers and millers.

Brewing by the Watney family began with this second generation in the late eighteenth century. They became corn factors and maltsters, with William, the eldest, the first to become a brewer, but this branch of the family had no connection with the Stag Brewery until long after the descendents of his youngest brother, John, had made their name there. John's son, James Watney, was born in 1800 and it was he that was to become the great brewer and founder of the Watney empire.

After the death, in 1788, of Edward Burnaby Greene, the Stag Brewery was to remain in the hands of Moore, Elliot and Co. for many years, slowly regaining some of its former reputation. John Elliot died in 1829 being succeeded by his eldest son John Lettsom Elliot, and, in 1831, he and Charles Lambert took complete control. Six years later James Watney joined them in partnership. By 1849 they were trading as Elliot, Watney and Co.

Elliot retired from active life in the brewery in 1858, and the name was changed to James Watney and Co., with the eldest son of James, also named James, joining the brewery and taking an increased interest in the art of brewing.

Two other London breweries taking an increasing share of the trade were Combe, Delafield and Co. at the Wood Yard Brewery and Reid and Co. at the Griffin Brewery. By the 1800s, Combe's were in fourth place in barrelage among London brewers, while Watney's and Reid's shared sixth place.

Since 1851, the year of the Great Exhibition, light pale beers had ousted other brews in the popular taste. At the Wood Yard Brewery, Combe, Delafield and Co. quickly adjusted their methods to meet the new demand. At the Stag Brewery, the tradition of brewing Pimlico or pale ales had survived the long ascendancy of porter and although, together with stout, this was still brewed, paler lighter beer represented the bulk of the barrelage. Reid and Co. at the Griffin Brewery, with their established reputation for stout, catered almost exclusively for that market.

The Stag Brewery 1880. *(courtesy: Courage Group)*

During the next twenty years, Watney and Co., under the guidance of the two James Watneys, progressed to the first rank of the great London brewers. The vigorous campaign prosecuted, at this time, by the teetotal movement, did not influence the good sense of the Englishman who still liked his glass of beer, whatever critics might say.

The first brewery taken over by Watneys was that of More and Co., then trading under the style of the Scottish Brewery in Old Street. This stood on the site of the first Samuel Whitbread's Goat Brewhouse, before his removal to the Chiswell Street site. Subsequent brewers had carried it on after Whitbread but with little success. Robert More rescued it from the doldrums and was followed by his son, John McLeod, who, on account of his Scottish extraction, gave it a new name.

The next step forward for Watney was the purchase of another brewery in Westminster itself. This was run by Carter, Wood and Co. and was known as the Artillery Brewery.

On July 8th 1898, three of London's brewing giants, Combe and Co., Reid and Co., and Watney and Co., amalgamated, with the joint capital fixed at £15,000,000, Sir Cosmo Bonsor, of Combe and Co., becoming the first chairman of the new Watney Combe Reid and Co. centred at Pimlico. Soon after the merger, Reid's Brewery was closed down, and in 1899 the greater part of the premises was sold to the London County Council who built a housing estate on the site.

Reid and Co.'s Griffin Brewery, early nineteenth century.   *(courtesy: Courage Group)*

Between 1901 and 1903, Watney took over control of the old Alton Brewery of Crowley and Co. and that of Harris's Knowle Green Brewery of Staines. At the sale of Chandlers Brewery in 1910, fourteen of their houses in Hastings were added to Watney's tied estate. The following year Bligh's Brewery of Sevenoaks was put up for auction, and twenty-seven more public houses were purchased.

During the years before the First World War, the annual output of Watney Combe Reid averaged one million barrels. Nevertheless, the many restrictions and trade difficulties greatly reduced profits. With only about five per cent of the public houses left free, brewers were no longer adding to their tied estate, so it was now more a question of improved brews and improved public houses to attract new customers.

In 1916, the transport problem, due to military requirements, became so acute, that the decision was reached to dispose of the old Taylor's Brewery at Saffron Walden (which Reid's had bought twenty years previously) to Benskin's Brewery of Watford. By this means, eighty or so houses in an isolated area passed out of Watney's possession.

1920 saw the Welch Ale Brewery of Kings Road, Chelsea being purchased. Originally founded in the mid-nineteenth century by John Bowden in the Fulham Road, just within the parish of Kensington, it became known as 'The Royal Brewery', presumably because it stood in a royal borough.

Before 1930 there were more important additions, first the Cobham United Breweries Ltd. (with thirty-three licenced houses), followed by the old established Isleworth Brewery of Middlesex, the Lion Brewery of Soho and the London and Burton Brewery of Stepney. The policy of ploughing back the profits into the business had enabled the company to purchase such small breweries from a reserve fund created for this purpose.

During 1930, Watney's were the first in the field with their research and experiments to produce what was originally known as 'container bitter', the forerunner of what later became known all over the country and extensively overseas as 'draught Red Barrel'.

The early fifties were particularly active with Watney's buying Hammerton and Co. of Brixton, thus acquiring two hundred off-licences, the public houses being sold to Charrington and Co. Two years later, the considerable brewery of Tamplin and Sons of Brighton, with four hundred licenced houses, became part of Watney.

For some years the board had been considering the future development of the valuable Stag Brewery site. After long deliberation it was decided that the brewery should be closed and that Watney should retain enough of the site upon which to build new headquarters offices, leaving the rest free to be leased for development purposes. Since the Mortlake Brewery was quite unable alone to meet the full demand for Watney beers, there remained two alternatives; either build another

The Stag Brewery
before demolition
in 1959.
(courtesy: Courage
Group)

brewery on the eastern side of London or to come to some arrangement with a brewery company already situated there. The second of these two alternatives was finally adopted, and Mann, Crossman and Paulin Ltd. were approached in 1958 with proposals for an amalgamation.

Mann's Albion Brewery at Whitechapel had been renowned for 150 years for high quality beers and had indeed introduced the first brown ale in bottles as early as 1899, the inspiration of Thomas Wells Thorpe, head brewer at that time. Negotiations were successfully concluded, which led to the combination of the two firms by an exchange of shares. Thus, the new company and style 'Watney Mann' was born.

Two of the original partners, Robert Crossman and Thomas Paulin, had been employed together as young men at the old Isleworth Brewery before joining the Mann family at Whitechapel. There was another link with the past, Brandon's Putney Brewery, which had bought the small Richmond Brewery of Daniel Watney, had itself become part of Mann, Crossman and Paulin some years earlier, and by this devious route, a brewing endeavour of an earlier date than that of Watney at the Stag Brewery became 'part of the family' again. The Albion Brewery had remained in the hands of the Mann and Crossman families ever since, although directors of both breweries joined the parent board of Watney

Mann Ltd. The separate styles of the two companies were continued for trading purposes.

April 23rd 1959 marked the last brew at the Stag Brewery after well over three hundred years of continuous production. It was also the end of brewing in the City of Westminster, where once so many breweries had prospered.

Watney's trading north of the Thames had been much extended by the amalgamation with Mann's, whose houses stretched as far north as Coventry, with quite a number of them in Luton. To overcome the problems of brewing and supply for this increased trade an amalgamation was concluded in March 1960 with Phipps Northampton Brewery Company Ltd. Two months later, a further step to secure brewing capacity outside London was taken by the amalgamation with Ushers Wiltshire Brewery Ltd. With nine hundred licenced premises, the brewery at Trowbridge was well positioned to support Watney's trade in the west of England. The third merger of that year occurred with the acquisition of Wilson and Walkers Brewery and their one thousand plus houses in the Manchester area.

Watney Mann came under the control of Grand Metropolitan Breweries during the 1980s, and in March 1991 a deal was struck with Courage Breweries whereby Grand Metropolitan ceded their breweries to Courage in exchange for 5,500 public houses and licenced premises. Courage now handle all the brewing at their breweries in Reading, Bristol, Tadcaster and Halifax.

CHARLES WELLS

Charles Wells was born in Bedford on August 13th 1842. He was the second son of George Wells, the proprietor of a furnishing business in Bedford High Street. Educated at the Commercial (Modern) School he left, aged fourteen, and went to sea, serving before the mast on various sailing ships owned by the Blackwall Frigate Company. From serving as Third Mate in 1861 to Chief Officer by 1868 he gained his Masters Certificate, being offered command of the first steamship built by his company.

His plans for marriage were thwarted when his prospective father-in-law told him that he would not permit his daughter, Miss Josephine Grimbley, to marry a sea captain who would be absent for so much of his time. He retired from the sea, married in 1872, and with help from his father purchased, in 1876, an old-established brewery in Horn Lane, Bedford.

A malthouse had existed on the site from at least 1744 when the River Ouse was opened to navigation. By 1762 barges from as far away as the Wash had access to the town, thus making easier the import of raw materials and the distribution of the finished product. Some time before 1836, the owner of the site, Stephen Benson, demolished the old malthouse and adjacent cottages to build the new Brewhouse.

When purchased by Charles Wells, the brewery consisted of a 'residence with garden and paddock' with two acres, a malthouse and a brewhouse with a five quarter mash tun, a fifty barrel iron liquor tank, a thirteen barrel open copper, a hop back cooler and refrigerator, tuns, pumps, horse wheeled machinery along with thirty-five public houses, most of them in Bedford and its surrounding area.

With a vigour which was to typify his long career in business and public service, Charles set about rationalising his new purchase, upgrading the brewery and licenced estate. By 1910 his base was secure and the now flourishing business made its first acquisition, the Cardington Brewery and chain of public houses.

Following his death in 1914 aged seventy-two, his sons continued to develop the business, by taking over other brewing companies in and around Bedford and by acquiring more public houses and developing existing ones.

In 1917 the Phoenix Brewery in Midland Road, Bedford, was purchased. This brought with it a substantial licenced estate trading under the 'Jarvis' banner. In 1919 and 1920 the estate expanded further with the purchase of the Newport Pagnell Brewery and tied houses, and a group of public houses from Day's Brewery in St. Neots. From there onwards the company concentrated on organic growth by seeking out sites for the development of new public houses, filling in logical gaps in a licenced estate which now totalled more than two hundred houses. In 1956 the third generation of Wells took over the helm and in 1963 the Abington Brewery of Northampton was acquired. The twenty-three public houses which came with this takeover meant that the company now owned 265 pubs – all within a forty mile radius of Bedford.

The old brewery was somehow still managing to sustain the estate, however at peak periods demand was now outstripping total production capacity. In a deal with the Borough of Bedford, a new site on the edge of town was exchanged for the old town centre property. On the new site an entirely new 100,000 barrel capacity brewery was built, starting in 1974 and completed in 1976, the company's centenary year, and opened by the Duke of Gloucester.

The move had immediately doubled brewing capacity, but continued investment into the licenced estate instigated further plant additions for ever increasing quantity and improving quality. Between 1987 and 1992 the brewing capacity again doubled to cope with the company's penetration into the take-home trade. Unusually for a brewery of its size, some fifty-five per cent of production is lager.

The present managing director is John Wells who is a fourth generation Wells. He was appointed High Sheriff of Bedfordshire, the third member of the Wells family to be honoured with the appointment.

After 110 years, the affinity between Bedfordshire and its local brewery is as strong as ever.

Charles Wells' Horn Lane Brewery.   *(courtesy: Charles Wells)*

WELLS and WINCH

In 1764 Samuel Wells, a brewer, purchased a house, brewhouse and maltings in Back Lane, Biggleswade. He later bought The Kings Arms Inn situated in the High Street; the building is now occupied by Lloyds Bank. He died in 1781 having purchased four more public houses and was succeeded by his son Samuel who continued to buy property and land so that he could extend the brewery. Biggleswade, being a stopping place on the Great North Road, was handily placed for trading in beers and spirits and it is no suprrise that the business thrived. Samuel built the two main coaching inns in the town, namely The Swan Inn and The Crown Inn. Upon his death, in 1831 aged seventy-six, the firm of Wells and Co. included forty-six public houses, several maltings and the Biggleswade Bank. The brewing business alone was valued at £48,000.

Two of his sons-in-law Robert Lindsell and William Hogge carried on trading as Wells and Company and continued buying public houses and property. 1840 was a particularly good year as they purchased eleven premises from John Day of St. Neots, thus extending their trade into that territory. Descendants of the two partners ran the ever expanding business until it was put up for auction in 1898 whereupon it was sold to George Winch for £55,000, the new company being named Wells and Winch Ltd.

George Winch and his brother Thomas were the sons of Edward Winch, who had leased a brewery in High Street, Chatham in 1851. Thomas had trained as a brewer at Morgan's Brewery in Norwich and took charge of the Chatham Brewery after his father's death in 1885. His brother, a solicitor, involved himself in the business. Together they purchased the brewery in 1891 forming Edward Winch and Sons Ltd., before merging with A. F. Style and Co. of the Medway Brewery, Maidstone in 1899. They changed their trading name to Style and Winch Ltd. based at Maidstone.

After his acquisition of the Biggleswade Brewery, George Winch in his capacity as Chairman of the new Wells and Winch Ltd., gave a dinner to all of their tenants in April 1899 where he was well supported by the rest of his board. The new owners were well received by the tenants and employees, especially as each year the workers were treated to an excursion to the seaside, alternating between Yarmouth and Skegness. At Christmas, each married employee was given 6lbs of beef, single employees 3lbs of beef, with the office staff each receiving a turkey.

Surplus property, not connected to brewing, was sold off to raise capital for expansion. From 1899 to 1903 the brewhouse was completely rebuilt and new machinery installed.

The first expansion of the new Company came in 1900 with the purchase of Henlow Brewery belonging to John Brown Staines Holden. The price was £9,585 and with it came ten public houses and a trade of one thousand barrels per annum. This was followed by the purchase of the Baldock Brewery in 1904 with twenty-two licenced houses, three of them in London, and a trade of three thousand barrels.

Beers brewed at Biggleswade at that time were – XX and AK mild and IPA bitter. In 1907 Stingo was introduced and sold until 1963.

The arrival, in 1912, of thirteen special trains full of troops to be billeted in Stratton Park during Army manoeuvres, boosted trade considerably. The first weekend after their arrival the brewery requisitioned thirty carts from local firms to ferry supplies of beer and ginger beer to the thousands of thirsty soldiers.

The London manager of Style and Winch was Alfred John Redman, who had served his apprenticeship at the Priory Brewery, St. Neots. He was invited by the Winch family to work at the Biggleswade brewery for two days per week and to advise on business matters. Just six weeks after this invitation he was made Managing Director with George Winch as Chairman.

A print from the architect's plan for the new Wells and Winch Brewery 1901.
(courtesy: Greene King)

An auction held in November 1919 saw the sale of the Priory Brewery to Wells and Winch for £40,000, which included thirty-four licenced houses and nineteen beerhouses. Half of the pubs were then sold to Charles Wells Ltd. of Bedford. From 1921 to 1923 Wells and Winch purchased two more brewing concerns. First was the Ashwell Brewery of J. R. Page and Co., adding twenty-six public houses, followed by the Bedford brewery of Newland and Nash Ltd. for £100,000. This now gave Wells and Winch control over their eighty-two pubs (seventeen in Bedford) and an annual trade of 15,000 barrels.

After increasing the brewing and fermenting capacity at Biggleswade, the Bedford plant was closed which resulted in the doubling of output and trade at the home base. Capacity in 1930 was up to almost 38,000 barrels and net profits just over £31,000. They controlled almost three hundred public houses, only two of them in Luton, they being *The Jolly*

Topers at Round Green and their flagship *The Midland Hotel* in Williamson Street.

1938 was particularly busy, with the acquisition of the Mill Bridge Brewery in Hertford for £21,000 and the Cambridge depot of Barclay Perkins and Co. Ltd. for £128,000. These two purchases brought in thirty-four pubs and yearly turnover of 6,000 barrels. This year saw the peak of Wells and Winch's fortunes with 383 public houses serving eight counties. Of the 220 in Bedfordshire there were still only two in Luton. They controlled the largest tied estate in Bedfordshire, the other two remaining breweries, J. W. Green and Charles Wells controlling 320 and 200 respectively. Their trade had now increased to 57,000 barrels but they were outsold by J. W. Green, possibly because of Luton's concentration of thriving pubs.

Much building improvement was carried out on the brewery site and new vehicles purchased for the transport fleet. A few dray horses were still retained, mainly for use on local deliveries.

The Company saw the war out well, even with the shortage in beer and the problems of maintaining the transport fleet. Immediately after the war, with 378 houses under their control, the annual production reached the record high of 89,736 barrels. From this peak the turnover and fortunes of Wells and Winch slowly began to decline. In 1957 Whitbread and Co. purchased ten per cent of the ordinary shares, a move that the board did not object to, reasoning that other potential bidders would be put off. At about this time Whitbread's also acquired a similar holding in Flowers Breweries Ltd. of Luton.

During the early 1960s the National Brewing Groups were being formed, which severely affected the smaller breweries who found that they couldn't compete with the huge advertising campaigns launched by the big brewers. With trade dropping below 40,000 barrels, the board of Wells and Winch began to look around for another brewery to merge with. Colonel Jack Redman opened discussions with Greene King and Sons Ltd. which were to prove beneficial to all concerned. The agreed merger terms were that Greene King offered to purchase all the share capital on an exchange basis of one Greene King ordinary share for every Wells and Winch share and equalisation for preference shareholders. The merger finally took place during 1961. Jack Redman joined the board of Greene King and Sons Ltd. His son Simon was appointed to the Wells and Winch board after having joined the Company as Outside Manager the previous year.

WRIGHT'S of WALKERN

Founded by Samuel Wright who started his brewing in old farm buildings. In the 1860s the brewery was destroyed by fire and a Hitchin diarist George Beaver recorded that 'Wrights brewery was burnt to the ground and the bursting vats sent volumes of beer down the road. Down went the good people of Walkern upon hands and knees and . . . well, all of that beer was not wasted'.

A new brewery was built and Samuel Wright continued to run it until his death around 1874. His executors J. Bullen and the brewer James Holland carried on with the business until Samuel Wright's sons S. and H. Wright took over and modernised the building, trading as Messrs. Wright and Co.

They converted the barley in their own maltings which consisted of a barley loft, steeping cistern, two growing floors, 40 feet by 150 feet, a drying kiln and a malt store. Later, in 1907, the site also included a cask cleaning department, a bottle washing department, engine house, stables, stores, hop room and mineral water factory. They made aerated water in bottles and syphons as well as dry ginger ale. These became so popular that they took over from beer brewing. Beer production ceased in 1924 when their twelve pubs were sold to the Simpson brewery in Baldock. In 1955 cider production also ceased and Wright's concentrated on making soft drinks.

THE PUBS

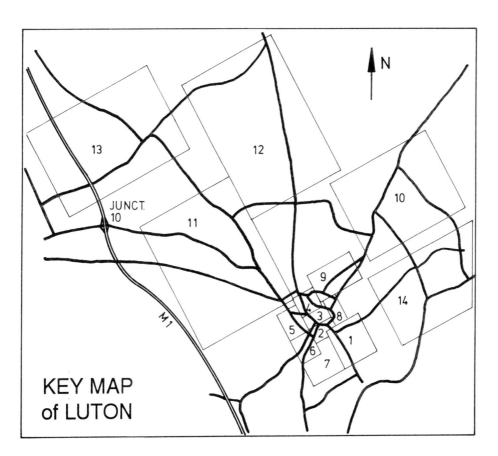

N

JUNCT.
10

M1

KEY MAP
of LUTON

1 Park Street and South New Town
2 Park Square and Market Hill
3 George Street and Central Luton
4 Manchester Street & Upper George Street
5 Stuart Street and Chapel Street
6 Castle Street and Windsor Street
7 Latimer Road and New Town Street

8 Church Street and Bute Street
9 High Town
10 Round Green and Stopsley
11 Dallow, Dunstable & Leagrave Roads
12 Biscot and Limbury
13 Leagrave
14 South East Luton

PARK STREET
and
SOUTH NEW TOWN

A visitor arriving in Luton from the south, during the early years of this century, had a choice of two routes into the town, London Road and Park Street. Most through traffic would choose the London Road, mainly for the convenience of good roads and the availability of transport. A traveller's first sight of the town, having chosen to journey from the villages in the south, would be the area now known as Park Street, previously called Sheep Street, because of the sheep fair once held there, Park Road and also South Street.

This area had been the host to Luton's street market and 'stattie' fair before the market moved up to ply its trade on Park Square. The abundance of public houses can be explained by the necessity to support the market trade and the mushrooming population of the newly built district of 'Brown Brick' which was to become New Town. Development had started during 1841 and by the end of the century many of the properties were already showing their age and being classed as slums, not fit for habitation.

Park Street and the adjoining part of New Town, have suffered twice from wholesale demolition. In the first instance, the German Luftwaffe were responsible for causing much damage in August and September 1940. The August raid was aimed at the Vauxhall Works with Park Town suffering badly as the aircraft continued to drop their bombs as they flew away from their target. The September raid included a 1,000 kilo. bomb hitting the bus station in Park Street and destroying many properties in the immediate area with a high casualty figure. The Parkway service station and adjoining flats were later built on the site of the destroyed houses and shops. *The Goat* public house received severe damage although not enough to warrant its demolition.

The second important clearance programme occurred during the early 1970s, when much of the west side was demolished to provide new housing and to accommodate the building of the Park Street end of the Luton by-pass, resulting in the loss of five public houses.

The visitor of 1900 would have had a choice of eighteen pubs in which to have 'whet' his whistle, compared with today's customer who would find a total of eight, one of which has only recently opened its doors to the paying customer.

1 Maud Gonne's, 202 Park Street

Built around 1855 and originally called *The Heron*, it was granted its first licence within the year and one of the first tenants was James Parrott, shortly followed by Thomas H. Moscrop. The pub was owned and supplied by Thomas Sworder of the Crown and Anchor Brewery.

During its early years the pub played a part in a particularly brutal and callous murder which shocked and angered the local community. In 1857, a young malt-maker from Ware, Hertfordshire, by the name of Joseph Castle, married a nineteen year old quiet, studious girl who lived with her family in York Street, Luton. The marriage of young Jane Whitcroft to Joseph Castle was doomed from the start. He was a moody heavy drinker who often beat his wife when he was drunk. After one such experience, Jane decided to leave the marital home in Ware and walked the twenty-four miles to her parents' home in Luton, followed the next day by her husband. After spending the night at *The Windmill Inn* in Kimpton Road, he arrived at York Street on the morning of August 9th 1859. He pleaded with his wife to return with him and threatened her with dire consequences if she refused. She agreed to join him and they set out for Ware.

Within the hour Joseph Castle had reverted to form and was ill-treating his wife. By the time they were passing *The Windmill*, the landlord was attracted by the sound of a woman crying and was later to tell the court of the man's savage bullying and demented nature. Within a mile of the pub, on the path that led to Chiltern Green *via* Someries Lane, Castle attacked his wife with a knife and hacked her to death. He dumped the body off the path into a chalk pit and continued on his way.

Her body was found shortly afterwards by a groom employed at Someries Farm. He returned with a horse and cart to convey her body back to Luton. In those days public houses often served, amongst other uses, as mortuaries and so he drove to *The Heron*. Her body was carried into the stables and the police were informed. A posse was formed, and with three bloodhounds from the Luton Hoo estate, set off in pursuit. This was the first occasion in this country that bloodhounds were used in an official man-hunt. After finding the murder weapon at the scene of the crime the dogs took up the scent, and a few hours later Joseph Castle was captured at Welwyn, Hertfordshire.

After admitting his guilt he was taken to *The Heron* and shown his wife's body, while efforts made by the assembled crowd outside to secure and lynch him there and then were quelled with difficulty by the police. He was lodged in the local gaol throughout the night, and after several attempts by the crowd to burn down the gaol, reinforcements were called in from Bedford whence he was escorted and put on trial. He was found guilty and duly hanged on the last day of March 1860.

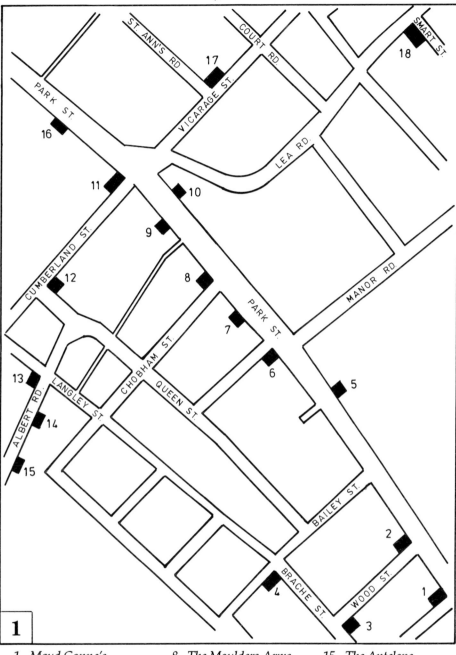

1

1	Maud Gonne's	8	The Moulders Arms	15	The Antelope
2	The Goat	9	The Four Horse Shoes	16	The Chicago
3	The Cardinal	10	The Wheelplough		Rock Cafe
4	The Volunteer Inn	11	The Luton Pier	17	The Hearts of Oak
5	The Falcon Inn	12	The Blue Lion	18	The Lea Bridge
6	The Chequers	13	The Windsor Castle	19	The Windmill
7	The Bat and Barrel	14	The Angel		(not on map)

This was one of the last public executions to take place at Bedford.

To celebrate his execution, the people of Luton lit a huge bonfire in George Street and sang and danced around it until the early hours of the morning. Souvenirs in the form of lace bobbins, suitably inscribed with Joseph Castle's name and year of execution, were passed round to the assembled throng. Several of these bobbins are now in the Luton Museum.

Public hangings often aroused popular interest and the following verse was printed on broadsheets and appeared at the execution:

> *A young man here in the prime of life,*
> *By evil passions onward led,*
> *To murder her he vowed to love,*
> *and at the sacred altar wed.*
>
> *On the high road, he took her life*
> *with instrument they used at meals,*
> *dreadful to think, – a table knife.*

From 1897 the pub, by now renamed *The Blacksmiths Arms*, came under the ownership of J. W. Green subsequently being owned by Flowers, Whitbread and currently Courage. The building was considerably reconstructed between the wars and underwent further extensions, on the town side, between 1969 and 1973. A busy friendly pub that has featured live music for many years.

During the early part of 1994 the pub underwent a complete face-lift under the watchful eyes of licensees Liam and Geraldine McNally who took it over on March 16th 1994 and reopened with an Irish theme and a new name – *Maud Gonne's*, after an Irish lady who, it is said, inspired the love poems of William Butler Yeats. Mr McNally had an unusual sending-off for *The Blacksmiths Arms* name. In June 1994 he held a wake for the old pub, and invited all his regulars to attend dressed in mourning clothes. A coffin took pride of place in the bar and was tried for size by some enterprising customers. The house now displays work by Irish artists and features traditional Irish music.

2 The Goat, 182 Park Street

Built at the same time as *The Blacksmiths Arms* and in 1876, under the ownership of Thomas Sworder, the tenant was Charles Parrott. This man possibly could be a descendent of Robert Parrott, the master brewer at *The Wheelplough* brewery further up Park Street. It suffered damage from an air raid in 1940 and was finally demolished in 1974.

3 The Cardinal, 6 Brache Street

Licence first granted in 1865 and owned by John Steed of Baldock. Steed died in 1877 and his son Oliver succeeded him until his death in 1888. The family sold out to the Pale Ale Brewery owned by William Pickering and purchased, in 1904, by Wells and Winch. In 1889 the pub was leased to J. W. Green by Mary Durrant a Luton widow.

In 1916 the building was rebuilt on the original site and in 1951 was purchased by Benskins who continued to operate the house until its demolition in 1972 due to the Park Town redevelopment. From 1942 until his retirement in 1958, Mr Frederick Ashpool was the tenant, the previous landlord having hanged himself in the pub cellar. This was the author's local from the mid 1960s until its demise.

4 The Volunteer Inn, 23 Bailey Street

Built in the 1860s and had its first licence granted in 1865. By 1876 it was under the ownership of William Barrett of Luton and occupied by George W Cooper. Tenants over the years have included Henry Sear in 1933, Walter Brown in 1950, Horace Lewis in 1960 and Joan Murry who was in occupation when it was demolished in 1972.

5 The Falcon, 119 Park Street

The name of this inn could have been derived from the sport of falconry, but it is possible that it has heraldic connections. It was the crest of Queen Elizabeth the First and also a sign of the Yorkist side during the Civil War.

In the 1876 licence returns the owner is shown as Sarah Heston of Luton but the leaseholder was J. W. Green, one of his first public houses. The building had been standing since at least 1855 and was the first pub in the town to run a slate club for its customers.

It closed for business in the late 1930s, and soon after was opened as a builders and calor gas dealers by Robert Colin Large who was to become Mayor of Luton (1950–1951). It remained as such until the 1970s, when the building was taken over by a tool hire firm and remains to the present day.

When under the ownership of Robert Large it was still possible to see fragments of the old pub internally but after being extensively modernised by the tool hire company all vestiges of the old *Falcon* have disappeared.

6 The Chequers, 112 Park Street

In 1794 an ancient inn named *The Chequers* stood in Park Street. It was kept by Mr Clarke in 1806 and later by William Tyler. The present inn certainly isn't that old but it is possible that it was rebuilt on the same site around 1850 when one of the first tenants was John Marston.

The name derives from the Roman days when establishments dealing in refreshments and providing a game of chess for their clientele would advertise the fact by placing a chequer board outside the door. The Romans brought the idea with them to Britain and hence it has become one of the oldest pub names in the country.

During the middle ages a table, which was divided into squares and called an exchequer, was used by merchants for purposes of accounting and revenue.

7 The Bat and Barrel, 104–106 Park Street

This house was trading since at least 1860 under the ownership of Thomas Sworder. It was called *The White Lion* and would trade under this name for 130 years. It gained some publicity during the days of the Temperance Movement when the landlord of the day climbed to the top of his high-masted sign, glass of beer in hand, and toasted a march past of the local Temperance Society.

In 1904 the pub was sold to Charles Wells of Bedford, it being that brewer's only foothold in the town until 1930. After acquiring the house the brewery spent time and money on providing an internal and external renovation. Further renovations and extensions were carried out between 1961 and 1964. When the off-licence in Court Road closed, the business was transferred to this house and carried on trading alongside the pub. The space used by the off-sales department has now been incorporated into the main drinking area of the pub.

On 9th February 1993 the Shefford brewery of Banks and Taylor took over the pub, renaming it *The Bat and Barrel*, this becoming their third retail outlet in Luton. They wished to emphasise the traditional public house image to complement their range of real ales, and so treated the public bar to an overhaul. The carpets were taken up to leave polished boards, and the walls were adorned with posters and old photographs. Mr and Mrs Liam Donnellan were taken on as tenants and entrusted to build up a trade that had been in decline for a number of years. Over the following year, with the range of quality ale on tap and with the influx of new customers from the University of Luton, the pub thrived.

Unfortunately, the owners, Banks and Taylor, had some difficulty with cash flow, which resulted in the Official Receiver being called in. The pub reverted back to Charles Wells' ownership and Mr and Mrs

Donnellan were kept on as tenants to carry on the good work they had started. With their friendly and agreeable approach, there is no doubt that the pub will continue to increase trade and be very successful.

8   The Moulders Arms, 2 Chobham Street

The house was operating as an unnamed beerhouse by 1845, under the occupation of Mathew Tomalin. Early this century the brewers Watney Mann took over the premises and named the inn for the first time.

During the 1980s, the house was taken over by a local family and the former Decimo retail shop adjoining was converted into a club and incorporated into the business. It is currently (1994) closed and offered for sale.

9   The Four Horse Shoes, 80 Park Street

Received its first licence in 1858 and by 1876 the owner was William Newman of Luton. Its main claim to fame stems from a serious fire over eighty years ago when the house was owned by Messrs. Pryor Reid and Co.

The tenant on the evening of Friday 31st July was a Mr William Littlewood Clifford aged fifty-six. He and his wife Annie Emily had only been at the pub since May 20th having moved from Penge.

On the evening of the 31st only three customers had been in the pub and so when he closed at 11.00pm he checked the pub throughout and retired to bed. Two lodgers staying the night and his young six year old nephew were already asleep upstairs.

At 3.40am the landlord's dog woke him up by jumping on the bed and he saw the room was full of smoke. His wife ran to collect their nephew and wake the lodgers; with the child she then went to the front left bedroom window to which the lodgers, having escaped from the rear windows and found a ladder, climbed up and saved them. When asked by the firemen, who had just arrived from the Church Street fire station, of the whereabouts of her husband she replied that he had gone down to the bar to check the fire. By this time the ground floor of the pub was a raging inferno taking the fire brigade one hour before the flames were extinguished.

Upon searching the ruins the body of William Clifford was found by the rear tap room door having perished within two feet of safety. Alongside his body was a cash box from the till containing the night's takings, 10s 1/2d (0.50p).

When the debris had been cleared it was seen how fierce the fire had been. The public and private bars were completely gutted. All traces of the wooden bar and furniture were gone and the only sign that it had once been a public house were a few badly burned kegs of beer. The living room, kitchen and tap room were also severely burned.

The inquest, held at *The George Hotel* heard that Mr Clifford had died within feet of safety by suffocation from the smoke.

10   The Wheelplough, Park Street

This fifteenth century building was the inn that started the long chain of brewers that was to lead to the J. W. Green brewing concern. A brewery was started on the site in 1655 by James Wilkins and was to continue brewing beer until purchased by Solomon Burr who closed the brewhouse down to concentrate his brewing at the Park Square brewery. Thomas Brown was tenant in 1845.

The inn continued under the supply of Burr's, Sworder's and then Green's until it was closed around 1906. The building then housed a bakery until its demolition during the early 1970s.

11   The Luton Pier, 4 Cumberland Street

The public house that was the predecessor of this pub would have been almost two hundred years old. Austin records that in 1806 an inn named *The Bull* stood at the corner of Park Street and Cumberland Street. By 1876 the inn was trading as *The Black Bull*.

It is unusual that a manor the size of Luton has not had its heraldic arms recorded by an inn sign but maybe this did occur with *The Black Bull*. It was recorded in Craven's Directory that Lord Hoo had a daughter, Anne, who married Sir Jeffrey Boleyn, Lord Mayor of London in 1460, the dowry being the manor.

Tradition says that their great grand-daughter, Anne Boleyn, was born there. The coat of arms of the Bullen or Boleyn family displayed the heads of three black bulls and it is possible that *The Black 'Bull Inn'* is a lone survivor of a long-ago connection with the Boleyn's occupation of the manor.

The demolition of this inn was necessitated by the Luton Corporation's proposed road widening scheme at this traffic junction in connection with the major proposals for the ring road development. In order to develop the corner site it was agreed with Lloyds Bank Property Co. Ltd. to construct a building comprising a bank, shops, offices and a new public house. Work on the project commenced in October 1967 and the public house was opened on 6th May 1969.

Whilst the building was in course of construction the old *Black Bull* continued to trade, until 7th April when it closed and was quickly demolished.

The old sign depicted the conventional bull but in the treatment of the new public house it was decided to change to the Spanish fighting variety. The first licensee of the new pub was Mr Leslie Richardson who had previously been catering manager at Wembley stadium.

Since its reopening the house has changed names five times. It's been called *The Grapevine, The Grapes, Parks, The Cumberland* and currently *The Luton Pier*. New owners have recently (September 1994) taken over and it is rumoured that the pub is to have yet another change in name.

12   The Blue Lion, 23 Cumberland Street

Probably built around 1840 and by 1876 was occupied by Edward Green and owned by Thomas and John Edwards of the Redbourn Brewery. This brewery was taken over in 1882 by Benjamin Bennett. The last licensees were Bernard and Doris Taaffe. It was demolished in 1970 to make way for the ring road development.

13   The Windsor Castle, 12 Albert Road

Built in the 1840s, and was first called *The Roebuck*. During the late 1850s the inn had many problems with the conduct and reputation of its clientele, exacerbated by the violent conduct of the former landlord towards his estranged wife who had retained the tenancy. It was an early acquisition of Thomas Sworder, going through the hands of J. W. Green, Flowers and Whitbread until changing hands in 1990 and now owned and managed by Charles Wells of Bedford.

Mrs Doris Taaffe was the landlady here after leaving *The Blue Lion* until her retirement in December 1987. She was followed by Mr L. Dalgarno, current owner of *The Wheelwright's Arms*. The present tenant is Nick Taylor, but he is due to leave the premises in July 1994, having been there since 1991.

14   The Angel, 29 Albert Road

There is very little recorded information about this house except that from 1869 to 1875 Eli Peach was licensee, with the owner listed as Maria Knight. It was perhaps one of the many beerhouses that sprang up during the latter half of the nineteenth century, remaining open but a few years. Certainly by 1876 there is no mention of it in the Luton licence returns.

15   The Antelope, 51 Albert Road

An early Thomas Sworder public house and one of the first occupiers was Lucy Gibbs. It is possible that Sworder purchased the premises on 26th September 1862 as the estate of the late Mr G. Haywood was sold at auction in *The Crown Inn*. The estate included *The Antelope* 'a public house with gateway entrance from the street and possessing a skittle alley'.

It was demolished between 1967 and 1968.

16   The Chicago Rock Cafe, 46 Park Street

One of Luton's newest licenced premises, one of a chain of these typically 1990s style *'theme venues'*. Features much Americana in the form of American automobile parts, hub caps, licence plates and photographs. Very popular with the young set and its turnover in various brands of lager far exceeds that of the traditional beers. Previously the site was occupied by a large building housing the business of C. W. Jones, a butcher and cooked meat tradesman. When it was demolished in 1973, Bejam, the cold food chain of stores, built the present premises. After the food store moved across Park Street the building was altered and *The Chicago Rock Cafe* opened in 1989.

17   The Hearts of Oak, 2 St. Ann's Road

Built between 1890 and 1900 when the dwellings in Vicarage Street, St. Mary's Road and Lea Road (formerly Blackwater Lane) were constructed. It was therefore a brand new building when J. W. Green added it to his growing list of tied houses. A typical late Victorian designed public house. Lasted only six decades before being pulled down in 1964 and replaced by the Luton Youth House.

18   The Lea Bridge, 108 Lea Road

Was built and opened at the same time as *The Hearts of Oak* but a much larger building than its contemporary. The licence was transferred from *The British Queen* that had stood in Bute Street. *The Lea Bridge* attracted most of its trade from the local residents of the Lea Road and St. Mary's Road area and consequently started to decline in the late 1950s when most of the nearby terraced streets were cleared for redevelopment, although it was many years before rebuilding started. It finally met its match in 1973 when the eastern end of the ring road was built. The site of this public house now lies in the car park directly below the eastern ramp of the flyover.

19   The Windmill, 93 Windmill Road (not on map)

Was trading on this site as long ago as 1855 and would have been named after one of Luton's windmills that stood close by on the Brache (now Vauxhall Motors sports ground). The old post mill had belonged to Mr R. Brown and had blown down during a hurricane on 19th December 1845, fatally injuring a man working in the mill.

At the time of its opening it was at the extreme southern end of the town. The main trade would have been from local farm workers, whose cottages lay close by, and as a stopping point for travellers on the Luton to Kimpton and Luton to East Hyde roads. The landlord provided stabling at the rear of the inn and in recent years these have been demolished to improve the customer car parking.

The building was extensively enlarged and renovated during the 1920s. A very popular public house, especially on working day lunchtimes with its customer base from many of the local industrial units and personnel from Vauxhall Motors.

It has recently, (1994), been altered internally by the owner Frederick King, who also owns *The First and Last* public house in Stopsley. Since this last revamp, the evening trade has considerably increased and it is crowded on most nights.

map ref. 1   *The 'Old' Blacksmiths Arms, c. 1910*

The Blacksmiths Arms, before the extension, c. 1965
map ref. 1   *(courtesy: Home Counties Newspapers)*

The Goat, c. 1965. Demolished 1974.   *(courtesy: Home Counties Newspapers)*
map ref. 2

The Cardinal 1930. Demolished 1972.   *(courtesy: Benskins)*
map ref. 3

The Volunteer Inn, 1967. Demolished 1972.   *(courtesy: Home Counties Newspapers)*
map ref. 4

Park Street and the Falcon Inn, c. 1934.   *(courtesy: Ken Cooper)*
map ref. 5

map ref. 5   *The Falcon Inn, c. 1935. It was to close within five years.*

map ref. 5   *Park Street 1994. This building once housed The Falcon Inn.*

The Chequers, c. 1953.   (courtesy: Colin Glover)
map ref. 6

The Wheelplough, c. 1906. Closed, c. 1906. Demolished 1970.
map ref. 10

The White Lion, c. 1953.   *(courtesy: Colin Glover)*
map ref. 7

map ref. 7   *The Bat and Barrel 1994.*

The Moulders Arms, c. 1953.   *(courtesy: Colin Glover)*
map ref. 8

map ref. 8   *The Moulders Arms 1994. Standing empty and for sale.*

map ref. 9 *The Four Horse Shoes 1908. The morning after the fatal fire.*

The Four Horse Shoes, c. 1953.
map ref. 9

(courtesy: Colin Glover)

The Black Bull, c. 1966. Demolished 1960.   *(courtesy: Home Counties Newspapers)*
map ref. 11

map ref. 11   *The Luton Pier 1994. The pub occupies the ground floor only.*

The Blue Lion 1966. Demolished 1970.   *(courtesy: Home Counties Newspapers)*
map ref. 12

The Windsor Castle, c. 1953.
map ref. 13

(courtesy: Colin Glover)

The Antelope 1955. Demolished 1967.
map ref. 15

(courtesy: Whitbread Archive)

map ref. 16   *Chicago Rock Cafe 1994.*

The Lea Bridge 1967. Demolished 1973.   *(courtesy: Home Counties Newspapers)*
map ref. 18

map ref. 17   *The Hearts of Oak 1958. Demolished c. 1964.*

The last tenant of the Hearts of Oak Mr W. Preece poses in the lounge bar.

map ref. 17

The Windmill, c. 1910.
map ref. 19

(courtesy: Frank Ludlow)

The Windmill 1958.
map ref.19

(courtesy: Home Counties Newspapers)

PARK SQUARE
and
MARKET HILL

Towards the end of the eleventh century, Luton comprised a small collection of wattle and daub houses with thatched roofs, clustering around the stone built church. Most of these houses were to be destroyed during the great fire of 1336 which burned the greater part of this, the ancient centre of the old town.

Many inns and taverns were built here to serve the growing town, and, as early as the fifteenth century, inns have found mention as standing in and around Church Street and Park Square.

Austin records several ancient inns, the exact locations not being known, but he did identify *The Barley Mow* as standing at the top of Church Street on the north side in 1850, it having been demolished by the end of the nineteenth century. The present day position for this inn would be in the vicinity of the new public toilets in Church Street.

From at least 1671 *The Cock Inn* has been resident on its site, *The Five Bells*, later *The Eight Bells*, dated from the fifteenth century. *The Rose and Crown* had mention in 1794, it possibly standing on Park Square, as was, in the sixteenth century, *The Royal Oak* and *The Vinecocks*, the latter having already disappeared by 1800.

In Common Street, which was the ancient name for the way from Market Hill to Park Square, was *The White Hart*, formerly *The White Lion*.

In 1869, on Market Hill, the exact position not known, was *The Grapes* beerhouse. The tenant, Mr W. Smith, advertised the fact in the Luton Times that he had taken over the premises and intended supplying every article in malt and spirituous liquors of the best quality and at the lowest prices. He was also to sell the 'choicest cigars'.

During the early 1900s, when Park Square was the setting for the open air market, the public houses of this district would have remained open for much of the day to supply the needs of the many Lutonians and visiting villagers that flocked into town on market day.

There has been a resurgence of trade, for these centrally positioned pubs, since the opening of the University of Luton, with the opening hours approaching those of ninety years ago.

1 The Cock Inn, 38 Park Street

In 1671, just six years after the great plague of 1665, *The Cock Inn* was getting its first mention, although there is a possibility that the inn

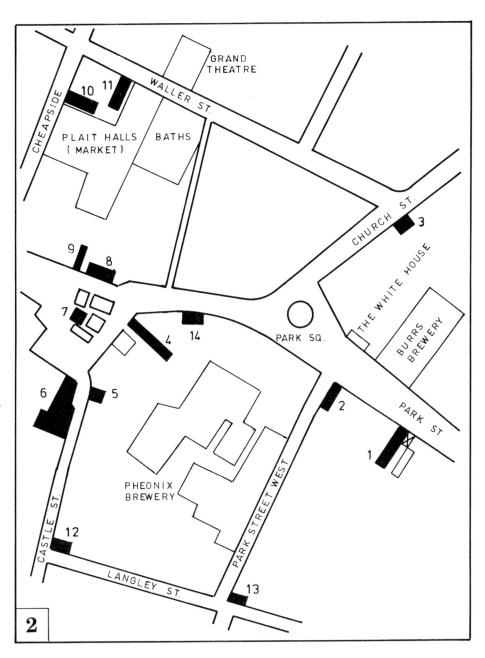

1   The Cock Inn
2   The Brewery Tap
3   The Wheatsheaf
4   The Rat and Carrot
5   The White Hart

6   The Red Lion
      Hotel/Brookes
7   The Kings Arms
8   The Black Swan Inn
9   The Plough

10 The Granville
11 The Panama Lounge
12 The Dog
13 The Greyhound
14 Yates's Wine Lodge

predates this mention. In 1759 it was sold to H. Bonner.

An old coaching inn, it was over one hundred years ago that the enterprising licence holder, farmer and carrier William Clarke, outdid all of the other coaching inns by completing the Luton to London trip and back in one day. The carriers from *The Shoulder of Mutton* and *The Two Brewers*, in order to compete, chased their customers aboard the coaches at five in the morning.

William Clarke, along with Thomas Sworder, was elected to the first Local Board of Health in 1850, this being the forerunner of the Corporation. At that time the Town Hall was owned by a private company who naturally charged a hire fee for the use of their building. Whether the company and the Board of Health didn't see eye to eye, or the Board wanted to conserve funds, they decided to hold their meetings at *The Cock Inn*; doubtless William Clarke provided refreshment at a profit. They continued to meet here for several years, even after their host no longer held an official position on the Board.

It was in this public house that the Burr family placed a brick of fired clay in the wall, from the deepest part of their new artesian well. Joseph Hawkes recounts that the brick had the date and depth of the well inscribed upon it and that it was placed over the door of the new club room. The brick is still visible over the door to the left hand room in the alleyway. Unfortunately the brickwork has been painted over but the name of Burr and the date can still be seen by those with good eyesight.

The building is two storeyed timber framed, reworked in red brick. A stable bar, separated from the main building by an old waggon way, was until recently used as an auction room but now is used for music evenings and as a function room.

2   The Brewery Tap, 22 Park Street

A timber framed building of seventeenth century origin. Before 1836 the original building, together with the ancient shop next door, formed part of the parish workhouse. After the workhouse was transferred to Dunstable Road the buildings were converted into private dwelling houses, still remaining the property of the Church. Earlier this century J. W. Green purchased the corner plot and opened the building as *The Brewery Tap*.

Until its major renovation in 1979, when the confectionary shop next door was incorporated into the premises, it had been an unattractive public house with a clientele mainly drawn from Luton's high Irish population.

It was one of the first houses to be treated to the 'theme renovation' and has since remained one of the most popular venues in the town.

3   The Wheatsheaf, 14–16 Church Street

An inn had stood on this site since 1798 when James Barett was the owner. Fifty years later Robert Dimock was the licensee and the owners were Messrs. Burr. The inn backed on to the Burr's brewery and no doubt was a popular delivery for the draymen, that's if Robert Dimock didn't collect his supplies himself. A painting by D. A. C. and E. K. Higgins completed in 1888 shows the building as a small rural type inn.

It was the only licenced house, in 1873, to have a court conviction against it but the cause of this fine has been lost in time. In 1876 it was owned by Thomas Sworder and occupied by Samuel Haydon.

The old inn was demolished in 1907 and the new building was only fifty years old when it was demolished in 1957 to make way for the new Luton College of Technology (now the University of Luton). The present site of the inn would be exactly by the Church Street side entrance to the University.

The sign of the wheatsheaf is quite a common inn sign and figures on the coat of arms of the Bakers Company. It has been recorded that many of the inns trading under this sign also baked bread on the premises, thus providing the two staple diets of the working man from one business.

4   The Rat and Carrot, 1 George Street

Formerly called *The Crown Inn* until the 1980s and then for a while *The Nickel Bag*, it occupies the site of the original sixteenth century inn. Austin recorded that 'Rychard Pygon, Yoman' was the owner in 1536–7. The present building was once part of a continuation of Middle Row from the Market House and led to Louse Lane and Pepper Alley. Later it became the entrance to Pearman's, later J. W. Green's, brewery. Middle Row, or what remains of it, is still visible for several metres until blocked by a brick wall alongside the pub. Not so long ago it continued for some way and provided parking for drinking customers.

It was at *The Crown Inn* that visiting Baptist ministers stabled their horses when attending the old Park Street Baptist Church. The elders most likely purchased the ale here, charged to church funds, which was provided for the town faithful, who would spend the whole day at the meeting house, bringing their own food. In 1845 the house was owned by the Burr brothers and occupied by James Burge. By 1876 he was still in occupation but by then he was also listed as the owner. Phipps Brewery of Northampton ran the pub until they amalgamated with Watney Mann in 1960. During the 1980s the house was renamed *The Heights*.

In January 1994 the pub was damaged when a fire broke out in a first floor office. The landlady, Marian Wallace, was rescued by a taxi driver who fortunately had been on the adjacent taxi rank. During January 1995 after further renovations the pub reopened under its present name and is now an extremely popular evening venue.

5 The White Hart, 1 Castle Street

Most public houses trading under this name have been influenced by King Richard the Second, as the White Hart was his favourite badge. The heraldic animal painted on the sign during the 1930s was shown wearing a collar. This stems from the legend that Diomedes consecrated a white hart to Diana, placing a collar of white gold around its neck. Many inn signs featuring a white hart show this collar or chain being worn.

In 1842 it was trading as a tavern, with Charles Squires as licensee, with a working brewery at the rear operated by Charles Hester. Situated on the main road in and out of town for London travellers and once called *The White Lion*, had to compete for customers with *The Red Lion* opposite, but the inn had no pretensions to being a coaching house. The famous Luton 'pudding stone' stood at the entrance to this inn's yard to protect the corner of the adjacent building from damage due to waggons and drays clipping the wall.

For some years it was owned by John Puddephatt before being purchased by Benskins. An attractive house that has the feature of a central bar surrounded by customers to all sides.

6 The Red Lion Hotel / Brookes, 2 Castle Street

The badge of John of Gaunt, Duke of Lancaster, was the Red Lion. He lived from 1340 to 1399 and it was during the next century that his badge began to appear on inn signs.

An inn has been on this site since the dissolution of the monasteries, one of the most ancient inns of the town. When the original inn was standing, George Street was a lane bordered by farms and meadows with the sheep fair in Castle Street just along the road. As road transport improved this inn became an important coaching house with stables for forty horses.

The inn stands on the site of the lodge of 'The Brotherhood House of the Guild of the Holy Trinity', a religious fraternity which supported a chapel and altar at the parish church. It is suspected that there may still be parts of the Brotherhood House incorporated in the present building, which was considerably rebuilt in 1881.

The first recorded tenant was John Smith in 1550 and one hundred years later a shortage of copper led to the landlord, Richard Hopkins, issuing his own tokens.

It was sold in 1759 to Richard Windmill and in 1806 was kept by William Green. In 1842 the Lucas Brothers of Hitchin were owners and suppliers to Robert Paybody, the occupier.

After being closed for much of 1994 while interior structural alterations were carried out, it reopened towards the end of the year with its new name. Fortunately the exterior remains basically unchanged and still sports the name of the Red Lion Hotel.

7   The Kings Arms, Market Place

Before the Corn Exchange was built in 1868, Market Hill was a ramshackle of old buildings and alleyways. One such alleyway, Middle Row, has already been mentioned in connection with *The Rat and Carrot* public house. At the George Street end of Middle Row stood *The Kings Arms*, previously called *The Half Moon*. Although built in the early nineteenth century an inn called *The Half Moon* had been on this site since at least 1706 when it was a brewhouse belonging to J. Marson. By 1842 the brewhouse had gone and the inn was supplied by the owners and brewers Messrs. Burr and they had installed Thomas Farmer as tenant.

The complete site, including the Corn Market House, was demolished in 1867 to make way for the Corn Exchange, itself demolished in 1951.

8   The Black Swan Inn, Market Hill

On the east side of Market Hill and dating from 1794. Fifty years later, in 1834, it was run by Thomas Tomlinson for the Burr Brewery. The inn was still trading until 1892 when the local family firm of Blundell's extended and took over the site. The structure of the building was retained but with a new facade. Blundell's store was to pass into history in 1978. The frontage of Debenhams store is now on the site of the old inn.

9   The Plough, 18 George Street

The Plough, as an inn sign, dates back to the times when most of the country earned its living by working on the land. During the middle ages, ploughs were blessed shortly after Christmas when a decorated plough would be used to raise plough-money to make a special plough-ale.

One of four public houses that were demolished due to the Arndale development in the 1970s. It stood three properties down from *The Black Swan Inn* and was built in 1833 when the owner, Richard How, was taken to court for obstructing the highway with his new building and cellar windows.

When it was demolished in 1973, some of the interior fittings were used by Luton museum to form the public house display in the Luton Life Gallery. The green tile relief, depicting a farmer's plough, from the front facade, was displayed as an interior decoration in the Debenhams restaurant until the restaurant was damaged by a fire and consequently the tile decoration was boarded up from view.

When it was learned that much of the town centre was to be swept away in the redevelopment, this pub became one of the most photographed buildings in the town; unfortunately other public houses that were threatened were not given the same consideration.

10   The Granville, 18 Cheapside

Opened around 1880 standing next to the Cheapside entrance of the Plait Halls (later the covered market) and was named after Lord Granville. Known as *The Plait Hall Inn* until a well liked character, Mrs 'Paddy' Bates, took over and prospered the house, along with the many charities she organised for the town. She adorned the walls with many photographs of music hall stars and numerous anecdotes of the stage, the Grand Theatre being only around the corner.

It was demolished in 1973.

11   The Panama Lounge, 34 Waller Street

As with *The Granville*, this pub also stood by an entrance to the Plait Halls. The house was opened around the same time as *The Granville*. It was for many years the only public house to bear a name connected with the hat industry, very fitting as it stood right at the heart of the hat trade area. The house was purchased by Thomas Washington Scott in April 1913, but it is not known when he vacated the premises.

A very popular pub during the 'swinging sixties', especially during Saturday lunchtime sessions.

It was demolished along with its close neighbour in 1973.

12   The Dog

An inn had traded on this site since at least 1806 when it was called *The Talbot and Dog*. At that time it was occupied by Mark Pates, and he was succeeded by his son, John. By 1876 it had been renamed *The Talbot* and owned by Thomas Sworder. During the early nineteenth century a bacchanalian drinking club, meeting under the name of the 'Soaksters Club', used the pub as its home base. Little has been recorded about this group of gentlemen topers except that the club had one rule only: 'No low quarrelling'! The club appears to have folded by the 1850s.

Austin records that in 1928 it was still trading as *The Talbot*, but shortly after, it was purchased by Benskins brewery who renamed it *The Dog*.

The talbot was a breed of hunting hound, now extinct, which was similar in appearance to the dalmatian breed, white with black spots all over its body and legs. The Talbot family, who were Earls of Shrewsbury, had the talbot as their crest. Many of the public houses still trading under the Talbot name are believed to have been named after this heraldic source.

In 1967 it was compulsory purchased by the Corporation for £20,130 which included the tenant's compensation. It was demolished later that year in a clearance programme for the inner ring road development.

13   The Greyhound

Built about 1870 by Thomas Sworder when Park Street West was laid out, and first occupied by Martha Wheatley.

Under the tenancy of Mr S. G. Rosson during the 1950s and 1960s it was often amongst the prize winners for the annual J. W. Green and Flowers licenced houses flower displays, where it featured strongly in the floral window box section.

It was demolished in 1968 when the site was purchased by Dunham and Haines to enable them to build an extension to their garage and show-rooms. The site is presently occupied by Courts Furnishing showrooms.

14   Yates's Wine Lodge, Park Street

The newest licenced premises in Luton, having been opened on 8th June 1994, during the writing of this book. It features the distinctive Yates's look with its bright atmosphere and elegant turn of the century design. Behind an impressive bar there is much gleaming brass and copper piping.

Yates's own fortified wines, including the famous Yates's Original Australian White Wine, are sold direct from the barrel.

The founder of the company, Peter Yates, launched his first Wine Lodge in 1884, in the north of England and the company has now spread its wings to most of the major towns and cities in the country.

Possibly one of the busiest and most popular evening venues in the town centre since the opening of the University of Luton.

map ref. 1   *Park Street during the 1920s, showing the Cock Inn.*

The Cock Inn, c. 1953.   *(courtesy: Colin Glover)*
map ref. 1

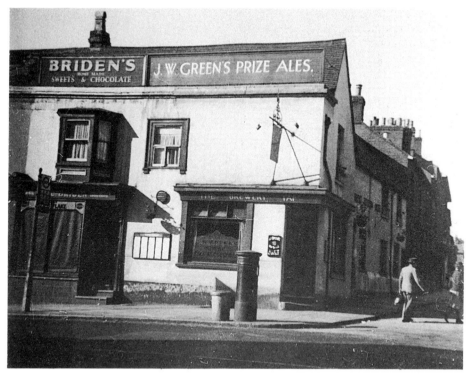

The 'old' Brewery Tap, c. 1953. Built on the site of the Parish Workhouse.
map ref. 2   *(courtesy: Colin Glover)*

The Brewery Tap in 1964, Before Renovation.
map ref. 2

map ref. 2   *The Brewery Tap 1994.*

map ref. 3   *The Wheatsheaf 1957. Shortly before demolition.*

map ref. 4　　　*The Nickel Bag, c. 1988. Formerly The Crown.*

The White Hart, c. 1930.   *(courtesy: Benskins)*
map ref. 5

map ref. 5   *The White Hart 1994.*

The Red Lion Hotel, c. 1955

map ref. 6   *The Red Lion Hotel 1994. Undergoing a refit.*

The Kings Arms, c. 1865. The complete site was demolished 1867.
map ref. 7

The Black Swan Inn. Shown adjacent to Blundell's. Closed in 1892 when Blundell's extended their shop.
map ref. 8

The Plough 1967. Demolished 1977. Some of the interior fitments now form part of the public house display in Luton Museum. *(courtesy: Home Counties Newspapers)*
map ref. 9

The Granville 1965. Demolished 1973.   *(courtesy: Home Counties Newspapers)*
map ref. 10

The Panama 1965. Demolished 1973.　　　　*(courtesy: Evening Post and Echo)*
map ref. 11

map ref. 12   *The Dog, c. 1930.*   *(courtesy; Benskins)*

The Dog 1953. View from Langley Street.   *(courtesy: Colin Glover)*
map ref. 12

The Greyhound 1960. Demolished 1968.   *(courtesy: Whitbread Archive)*
map ref. 13

Floral display at The Greyhound 1953.   *(courtesy: Colin Glover)*
map ref. 13

Yates's Wine Lodge 1994. Luton's newest public house.
map ref. 14

GEORGE STREET
and
CENTRAL LUTON

From the original town centre of Park Square and Church Street, the town began to grow northwards along George Street and as far as Bridge Street and Christ Church.

In the fifteenth century, George Street was a narrow lane of farms and fields, there being a farm close to the junction of George Street with Wellington Street as late as 1820, it having to be demolished to make way for the laying out of Wellington Street.

Some of the first buildings to be erected were the inns and brewhouses, there being a liberal selection of them at one time or another. Times have changed; of the eight inns shown on the map, only two survive, neither of them in George Street.

Four seventeenth century inns that have had a mention as being situated in George Street are *The White Horse*, which stood where Barclays Bank now is on Market Hill, *Fleur de Luce*, *The Windmill* on the corner of Chapel Street and *The Old Sergeant*, which Austin records as being opposite *The George Inn (Hotel)*.

There was once *The Old Tavern* in Adelaide Terrace, a particularly dirty, run down group of cottages that formed a court off George Street opposite *The Cross Keys*. The probable standards of hygiene and service in this alehouse, given the reputation of Adelaide Terrace, defy description.

As George Street continued to develop, especially after 1830 when the hat manufacturers began to build their factories and warehouses, the ancient inns surrendered to progress and very few survived into this century.

1   The Shoulder of Mutton, George Street

The origins of this inn sign derive from the publican having a second means of earning a living, namely butchering. Public houses bearing this name are quite frequent in the north of England. There is also one at Kempston-Green End.

The Luton inn of this name stood at the bottom of Market Hill close to the corner with Chapel Street. It was very ancient and probably, according to Austin, dated back to Tudor days. Beneath the inn were the last remains of the Shambles. It was pulled down on 1st August 1837 when it belonged to the Burrs, with the last tenant being William Goodspeed. Since then the site has been occupied by a fishmonger, a butcher, a tailor, not a candlestick maker, and currently by a flower arrangement shop.

2   The Old Bell, George Street (west side)

Perhaps the oldest inn known in Luton, finding mention during the reign of Edward the Fourth (1461–1470). At the beginning of the sixteenth century, during the reign of Henry the Eighth, William Child held the inn. Further mentions were in 1700, and between 1706 and 1711, when Trustram was tenant.

One hundred years later it was a malting owned by Robert Brown. It was almost certainly a victim of the development of George Street during the 1830s.

3   The Cross Keys, George Street

This inn, with a frontage of twenty feet three inches, was first mentioned in 1665 when some property was described as being between the Brotherhood House and the *Crosse Keyes Inn*. The next mention was on 14th July 1747 when purchased by Stephen and Elizabeth Chapman from James Crawley.

In the will of William Day, 1793, he left his wife, among other things, 'the messuage called *The Cross Keyes Luton*'.

On 1st May 1835 Cornelia Young and her sons leased the inn to Frederick Burr, common brewer, for six years, provided he repair and insure the premises for not less than £300 and maintain the premises as a public house. The lease was taken over in 1844 by Richard How, a victualler, of Luton, and he installed John Hawkes as tenant. It was occupied for a short time by Septimus Abbott before being purchased by Thomas Sworder. He leased it to Benjamin Bennett on a ten year lease and by the end of the lease Bennett was in partnership with a farmer of Tithe Farm, William Anstee.

The inn, along with the rest of Sworder's empire, was sold to J. W. Green before being put up for auction during the early 1900s, and finally demolished in 1905.

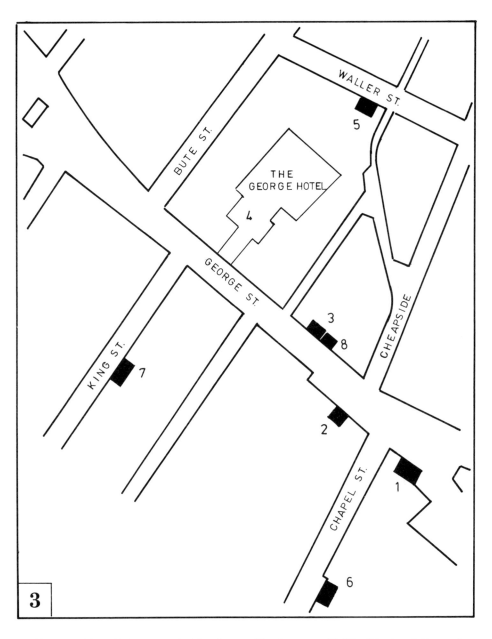

1 *The Shoulder of Mutton*   4 *The George Hotel*   7 *The Newt and Cucumber*
2 *The Old Bell*   5 *The George Tap*   8 *The Bell Hotel*
3 *The Cross Keys*   6 *The Bitter End*

4   The George Inn (Hotel), 52 George Street

Dating from the sixteenth century, it was undoubtedly one of the oldest inns of the town. By 1509 the inn was bearing its name, as we are told that Henry Stoppysley disputed with Thomas Thereder, a cordswain, and Thomas Woodward, a gent, and contested their holding '*The George*, its meadows and farmlands, oldtyme called *The George and the Swanne'*.

It once had an inn-sign on a beam of timber stretching over the narrow lane, which was then George Street; this sign was often set swinging by passing waggons if they were loaded too high.

The first landlord on record was one Staploe who died in 1680, the inn being taken over by his widow.

In 1781, the renowned Dr Samuel Johnson paid a visit to the inn. According to his biographer, Boswell, they 'visited the seat of Lord Bute on the King's birthday; we dined and drank his majesty's health at an inn in the village of Luton'. Lord Bute was of the family that occupied Luton Hoo from 1763 to 1844. It was during this time, in 1800, that *The George* featured in a riot between an army recruiting party and some resisting civilians when 'some damage was done'.

The coming of the modern age, the opening of the gasworks, was celebrated with an illuminated dinner and just two years later, in 1832, the proclamation of the young Queen Victoria was read beneath the Hotel's portals.

There was as stormy meeting held at *The George* in 1841, when the population of the town numbered almost 6,000. A proposition was being considered that the new London to Manchester railway should be built through Luton. George Stephenson himself was in attendance and he was amazed, then furious, when opposition to his railway developed. At the close of the meeting he proclaimed that Luton would never have a direct rail link with London for as long as he lived. Nor did it; he had died by the time the link was built in 1860. The tenant at the time of Stephenson's visit was Elizabeth Butlin and it was under the ownership of Richard Jones.

During its heyday there were stables for commercial and private carriages, which necessitated the front of the inn being altered to accommodate an entrance for traffic. When horses gave way to motorised transport *The George* boasted good garage standing. A further attraction for the customers was a well appointed billiards room with two tables.

Between the wars, dinner dances and public dances on Thursday and Saturday evenings were a very popular attraction. The main resident band, post war and until closure in July 1965, was Ken Green and his Orchestra.

5   The George Tap, 14 Waller Street

This public house stood alongside the rear garage entrance to *The George Hotel* and was affiliated to it for many years.

It was built on the site of the first building in Waller Street, a cottage belonging to the hotel, and had existed before the road was laid. It is interesting to note that, but for this building, Waller Street would have been made to run parallel and closer to George Street.

It was trading in 1895 and closed seventy-four years later in 1969, being demolished during 1971.

6   The Bitter End, 9 Chapel Street

An early nineteenth century town public house that is a grade 2 listed building. Until 1980 it had been called *The Griffin*. During the heyday of the Grand Theatre it was reputed that this establishment was the gathering place of the theatre crowd.

The building is unusual in that it is a three-storey house and still retains some remains of a cobble stone forecourt. A free house for many years and well known for its variety of real ales. Between August 1993 and February 1994, Mr Keith Gibbs was tenant. He has recently taken over at the *Old English Gentleman*. It is now owned by local businessman Brendan Sherry.

7   The Newt and Cucumber, 13 King Street

Had its first licence granted in 1863 and has been called *The Sugar Loaf Hotel* and later *Henekey's*. The original building only faced on to King Street with an open plot to the rear. It was extended rearwards around fifty years ago, and now has entrances from King Street and George Street West.

8   The Bell Hotel, George Street (east side)

Not to be confused with *The Old Bell* on the opposite side of the road. It first found mention in 1739 and by 1790 it was the overnight stop for the Ampthill to London coach. William Townrow was keeper of the hotel in 1806 but by 1876 it was owned and occupied by Sarah Puddephatt.

The building was considerably rebuilt around 1906, the new facade being basically as the building stands today except for the street level frontage.

It was closed at the end of the 1920s, having been owned and occupied since the beginning of the Great War by Daniel Millward.

The name is still visible today, high up on the upper storey.

A lithograph of Market Hill dated 1835. Shown, are The Kings Arms (centre) and The Shoulder of Mutton on the right side. The Shoulder of Mutton was pulled down in 1837.
map ref. 1

View of George Street 1855. From a lithograph. The Cross Keys is shown this side of the tall straw plait warehouse on the right side.
map ref. 3

map ref. 3   *The Cross Keys and The Bell Hotel, c. 1890.*   *(courtesy: Ken Cooper)*

map ref. 3   *The Cross Keys shortly before demolition 1903.*

George Street, c. 1910. The George Hotel on the right.   *(courtesy: Ken Cooper)*
map ref. 4

George Street and The George Hotel, c. 1914.   *(courtesy: Ken Cooper)*
map ref. 4

A promotional view of The George Hotel before the laying of the tram lines.
map ref. 4

Promotional views of the interior of The George Hotel during the 1920s.
map ref. 4   *(courtesy: Ken Cooper)*

map ref. 5   *Waller Street, c. 1910. The George Tap on the right.*

The George Tap, c. 1953.   *(courtesy: Colin Glover)*
map ref. 5

map ref. 6   *The Bitter End 1994. Formerly The Griffin.*

The Newt and Cucumber 1994. Formerly The Sugar Loaf and Henekey's. A view
map ref. 7   *featuring the King Street entrance.*

The Newt and Cucumber 1994. The George Street West Entrance.
map ref. 7

MANCHESTER STREET
and
UPPER GEORGE STREET

During the seventeenth century, the northern limits of the town reached to Bridge Street. The road to Bedford followed Manchester Street, and thence northwards to Bedford via Bridge Street.

There was at least one inn in this area at that time, *The Prince's Head*. Austin records that 'it was situated at the extreme limit of the town, near to the horse pool, at the corner of the road leading across the river on the way to Bedford'.

From at least 1842 until 1853, James Harris was landlord for the brewers Messrs. Burr and he honoured the Duke of Wellington by changing his sign to *The Duke's Head*. The building was later totally destroyed by fire. Many years later on the site stood the butcher's shop of Mr W. G. Durrant.

In 'The Story of Luton' we are told that in 1648 a considerable Royalist force hastily retreated through the town on its way to the north. A small party was delayed at an inn on the corner of Manchester Street, when they were surprised by troops of the New Model Army. There followed a short encounter in which six Royalist soldiers were killed and nine wounded. As *The Duke's Head* was trading in 1643 there is little doubt that this was the inn which witnessed the skirmish that took place five years later.

Three other inns have mention in the eighteenth century as standing in Manchester Street, *The Red Cow* on Tower Hill, *The Rose and Crown*, and *The Saracens Head*, both mentioned in 1794.

The streets to the north west of the Town Hall were mostly laid out after the Crimea War (1854–1856), hence the use of names such as Alma, Inkerman, Cardigan and Liverpool.

Thomas Sworder's brewery was in the area, as was one of his first acquisitions, *The Albion*, which no doubt played its part, along with the other pubs, in the mood changes, from jollity to frustration and anger, of the ordinary town citizens, who were later in the day, of 19th July 1919, set to riot and burn down the Town Hall in perhaps Luton's most notorious day in history.

1   The Belgium Arms, George Street

First found mention in 1847 and was adjacent to the old Town Hall. It was a tied house owned by Thomas Sworder until around 1872 when he sold it to Wells and Company of Biggleswade. They installed Frederick Rogers as tenant and in turn sold the premises to Roberts and Wilson of Ivinghoe in 1879. Eight years later the Corporation purchased the inn, closed it and incorporated the building into the Town Hall where it was utilised for the weights and measures department. In 1919 all remains of the old inn, along with the Town Hall, were destroyed in the fire following the Peace Day riot.

2   The Duke of Clarence, 1 Upper George Street

When first mentioned in 1771, Upper George Street was called Dunstable Lane. In 1806 this pub was kept by John Hill, followed by Martha Hill and went under the name of *The Two Brewers*, after malting partners who occupied the site when the duty on a barrel of strong ale was only 4s 9d. (24p). They were followed by John Burroughs, then John Hargraves for Messrs. Burr, and by 1876 it was owned by Thomas Sworder and occupied by Thomas Else.

It later changed to *The Clarence* before reverting back to its present name.

3   The Dew Drop Inn, 16 Upper George Street

One of three public houses owned in 1876 by Henry Fowler of Woburn and was later purchased by J. W. Green.

It was demolished in 1953 to enable the road to be widened, as the inn had been built when Dunstable Lane was a narrow thoroughfare. After demolition the site was taken up by an extension to the Town Hall. The licence was transferred to the newly opened *Wyvern Inn* on Eaton Green Road.

4   The Midland Hotel, 2 Manchester Street

A much larger premises when opened in 1868 than at its demise in 1976. It was owned by John Pugh of Windsor, a fact advertised with raised lettering above the upper storey. An extract taken from the Bedfordshire Times on 2nd July 1867 said 'A new hotel for Mr John Pugh is being built and will be called "*The Bedford*". It is expected to be completed in four months' time'. It added that the architecture of the new building

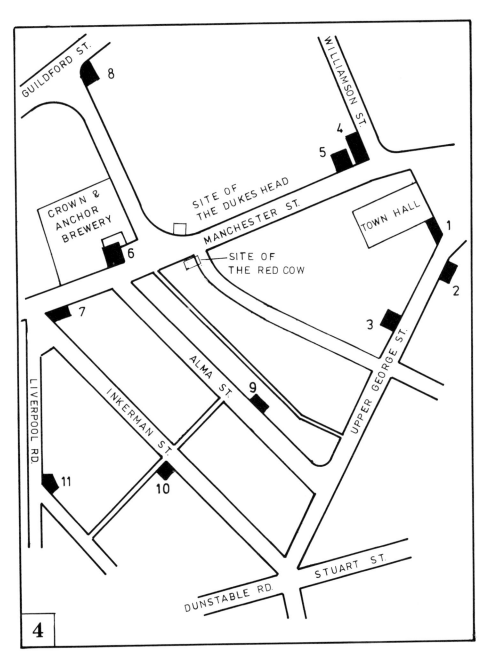

1 *The Belgium Arms*
2 *The Clarence*
3 *The Dew Drop Inn*
4 *The Midland Hotel*
5 *The Horse and Jockey*
6 *The Crown and Anchor*
7 *The Albion*
8 *Bridge Tavern*
9 *The Office*
10 *The Inkerman Arms*
11 *Shirley's Temple*

was to 'be in the Italian style'. This name was never used.

Sometime before 1928 much of the building was leased to an insurance company for use as offices and much of the ground floor to a ladies' gown shop.

The Hotel was purchased that year by Wells and Winch of Biggleswade occupying a lesser part of the building with an entrance in Williamson Street, some rooms still being available for rent on the first floor.

The bar was a popular meeting place for bus crews operating out of Williamson Street, while many passengers will tell of using it as a waiting room.

The complete building, along with the east side of Manchester Street, was torn down in 1976 to provide a temporary bus terminus on the site of what was to become St. George's Square.

5   The Horse and Jockey, 4 Manchester Street

A small inn had been on this site since the eighteenth century. Edward Smith, a farmer, was tenant in 1804 when he provided stabling for horses at the appropriately named *The Horse and Groom*. Sarah Higgins is listed as occupier during 1845.

The inn was owned and operated by Lucas Brothers of Hitchin until they were taken over by J. W. Green in 1921.

Old Lutonian Mr George Sibley, whose family ran the inn, recalled standing on the scaffolding, on Mafeking night 1896, when the inn was being rebuilt and renamed *The Horse and Jockey*. The new inn was not built exactly on the old site but set back from the street by ten metres.

A 1914 advertisement boasted that the inn offered 'two billiard tables, stabling for fifty horses and garaging for forty motors'.

The pub was closed for business in January 1960, when the Council paid £70,000 for it, and the licence and tenant transferred to *The Britannia* in Biscot Road. The front of the building was then extended forwards to the old building line and served until its demolition in 1976 as Chelsea Girl Boutique.

6   The Crown and Anchor, 2 New Bedford Road

Probably built around 1830 by John Gray at the same time as his brewery at the rear was erected. One of the first licensees was Joseph Everitt. It was purchased soon after by Thomas Sworder who made the inn and brewery the centre of his operations. The brewery was demolished in 1898, soon after it had been acquired by J. W. Green.

The public house plied its trade for many years after becoming a familiar site to Lutonians and travellers from the Hitchin area of Hertfordshire, as it featured as the terminus for the Birch Brothers' buses. In the 1960s, one of the strongest football teams in the local leagues used the pub's name and premises as its base.

Alongside the pub, with a frontage on Bridge Street, was a long red brick building used by the Luton Band as practice rooms. This building was all that remained of Sworder's brewery having been used as stables for his dray horses. 1975 saw the end of this historic little corner in Luton's brewing history when both buildings were demolished to be replaced by a couple of flower beds.

7 The Albion, 17 New Bedford Road

The inn sign represents the ancient and poetic name for England, and is gaelic in origin. Albion, so the legends tell us, was the son of Neptune and discovered England, ruling over it for half a century. Another story from the history books relates that Albion was a Roman, and after coming to England, converted to Christianity and became the first Christian martyr here.

The pub was built, circa 1869, owned and occupied by Charles Swain for the next twelve years. It was very possible that Swain ran a small brewhouse on the premises, this being converted into a mineral water factory when the site was purchased by Sworder. The house was sold to Green in 1897 and had previously been called *The Albion Tavern* and *The Albion Inn*, frequently causing confusion with the house in Ebenezer Street.

When it was decided by Luton Council to improve the Inkerman Street–New Bedford Road corner, the pub and its factory site were pulled down in 1969.

8 Bridge Tavern, 95 Guildford Street

Older than *The Albion* by about twenty years and was owned by Edward Taylor, although under lease to J. W. Green in 1876.

A large public house previously called *The Plume of Feathers*, also *The Studio*, under which name it was operated as a pub club, featuring heavy metal music. The clientele left a lot to be desired, and after being the centre of a fair amount of trouble and unrest it was closed down. It remained closed for eighteen months before reopening as *The Bridge*, with John Marshall as tenant. The interior was tastefully redecorated and it has now re-established itself as a friendly town centre pub. It is particularly busy on weekday lunchtime sessions. The name has been changed within the last two years.

9   The Office, 39 Alma Street

In its one hundred and twenty year history this pub has had three official names and one unofficial name by which most older Lutonions know it. It was first called *The Marquis of Bute*, after the Lord of the Manor. It was owned by the same man who also owned *The Dew Drop Inn*, Henry Fowler of Woburn.

A small terraced pub with split level bars, unusual in that the front door was approached by steps. More unusual was the rear entrance which gave rise to its most well known of names. Lancret's Path, an ancient alleyway connecting Upper George Street with Manchester Street, ran behind the pub and at some time the dividing wall had partially collapsed allowing access to the rear of the house. This gave rise to 'The Hole in the Wall' nickname which forever stuck. Later the damaged wall was repaired, a permanent gate being incorporated in it.

Later the name was changed to *The Cat's Whiskers* and of late to *The Office*, a handy excuse for a tired businessman, having a well earned drink at the end of the day, ringing home with the reason for his lateness 'sorry dear, I'm still at the office'.

The current tenant is Douglas Hay, who has been in charge for a year and a half. An attractive menu means that the busiest time for the pub is at lunchtime during the week.

10   The Inkerman Arms, 52 Inkerman Street

First licensed as an alehouse in 1874, although it was most likely built a few years before. This house was one of only two premises that the Hertford brewers McMullen and Sons have ever owned in Luton, the other property being a beerhouse in John Street. Within a couple of years even this small foothold of McMullen's had disappeared, because in 1876 this alehouse was under the ownership of Elizabeth Worsley of Luton. The John Street premises had most probably already gone, as no further record of it exists.

An ordinary end of terrace public house, very typical of the Victorian age. Later purchased by Thomas Sworder and passed to Green's in 1897. The pub was named after the battle of Inkerman during the Crimea War.

The current tenant is Mr Pat Coughlan, who has been in the business for twenty years, having been landlord at *The White Hart* from 1974 for five years, before taking over at *The Stags Head* until 1989. He has been at *The Inkerman* for the last six months (1994).

11   Shirley's Temple, 1 Liverpool Road

Built at around the same time at *The Inkerman Arms*, first named *The Bute Arms* after the Lord of the Manor. Originally owned by John Dear of Baldock, who was a brewery clerk at the Baldock Brewery in White Horse Street in 1853. He owned two public houses in the town and it is likely that he set himself up in the brewing business after learning his trade with them. There is no record of him owning a brewery, so it is more than probable that his supplies came from Baldock.

The pub was also called *Louis' Bar* for some time.

The Town Hall, c. 1880. The building to the left was trading as The Belgium Arms until around 1889. Thirty years later the site was destroyed by fire during the Peace Day riots of 19th July 1919.

map ref. 1

The Clarence Hotel, c. 1890. Peddars House on the extreme right was demolished in 1899.
map ref. 2

The Dew Drop Inn 1951. Shortly before demolition.
map ref. 3   *(courtesy: Home Counties Newspapers)*

The Midland Hotel and the original Horse and Groom, c. 1890. The latter was demolished in 1896 and rebuilt the same year. the Midland Hotel was demolished in 1976.
map ref. 4

The Horse and Jockey, c. 1953. Closed 1962 and the building
map ref. 5 *demolished 1976.*

The Crown and Anchor during the 1950s. At the rear of this pub, Thomas Sworder ran his brewery. The pub was demolished in 1975.
map ref. 6

The Red Cow on Tower Hill.   Position shown on map.

The Albion 1967. It was demolished in 1969.(courtesy: Home Counties Newspapers)
map ref. 7

map ref. 8   *The Plume of Feathers, c. 1955.*

The Marquis of Bute, c. 1953. Known as 'The Hole in the Wall'.(courtesy: Colin Glover)
map ref. 9

map ref. 9   *The Office 1994.*

map ref: 10   *The Inkerman Arms, c. 1953.(courtesy: Colin Glover)*

map ref. 10   *The Inkerman Arms 1994.*

The Bute Arms, c. 1960.   *(courtesy: Whitbread Archive)*
map ref. 11

STUART STREET
and
CHAPEL STREET

For centuries, Luton had consisted of three streets, Park Street, George Street and Church Street, with narrow lanes and ways leading from them. The housing that existed in this small central area during the early years of the nineteenth century was becoming more unsuitable in providing adequate shelter for the increasing number of people that were arriving in the town to seek non agricultural type work.

During the 1820s and 1830s there was much freehold property speculation in the New Town and High Town areas, where thousands of new houses were built, mostly without planning or adequate design, to meet the needs of the masses arriving in the town for work. These new properties themselves would be found to be unfit for human habitation within a matter of twenty years.

The majority of properties, covered in this section, to the west of Stuart Street, were built and completed between 1835 and 1850, Buxton Road and Rothesay Road being built during the following decade. This area of New Town, along with that to the south of Castle Street, boasted a great number of public houses and beer shops, particularly during the latter quarter of the century, providing much refreshment for the inhabitants of these densely populated streets. Only half of the public houses remain in business to this day, the lost premises mostly falling victim to the cull on beerhouses after 1869, the changes in leisure activities, the slum clearance programme and the inner ring road develop- ment of the late 1960s.

Whether it was the British public's preoccupation with Queen Victoria and royalty in general, or for some other reason, eight of the sixteen pubs, recalled here, have a royal connection in their original names, and six of them include the word 'Arms' in their title.

A beerhouse bearing a regal name was *The Prince of Wales*, which stood at the bottom of Regent Street on the town side corner. It was trading in 1864 and owned by John Steed of Baldock. It was last mentioned in 1907.

Two old inns to have traded in Wellington Street, and long since closed, were *The Eagle*, which stood on the upper corner of the junction with Peel Street, and *The Lamb* (see page 165). *The Eagle* was trading by at least 1865 and by 1876 had changed its name to *The Yorkshire Hotel*, when it was owned by James Darvell of Chesham and occupied by Peter Thornton. *The Lamb* was further up, on the south side, having earlier

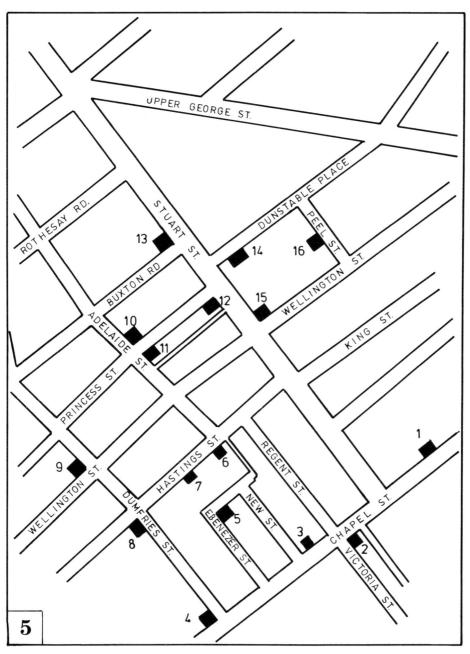

1 Rumours
2 The Queens Hotel
3 The Masons Arms
4 The Kings Arms
5 The Albion Inn
6 The Regents Arms
7 Monty's
8 The Two Brewers
9 The Fountain
10 The Princess Alexandra
11 The Star and Garter
12 The Duke of Edinburgh
13 The Bedford Arms
14 The Oddfellows Arms
15 The Wellington
16 The King Edward
    the Seventh

been called *The Wrestlers* or *Two Wrestlers*. This beerhouse had a very bad reputation amongst the law abiding citizens and with the police, whose headquarters were only a matter of a hundred metres away. The newspapers of the time were forever reporting cases brought against *Two Wrestlers* at the Petty Session Courts. The most frequent charges appeared to state that it was a clearing depot for stolen goods, as well as operating as a brothel. Historian Page Woodcock records that the site of this inn, or beerhouse, number 61 was later to be occupied by the Wellington cinema, since demolished and laying under the ring road. It is now known that the inn was at number 63 Wellington Street. The building is still standing and currently is used as a cafe. The inn ceased trading by 1869.

1   Rumours, 26 Chapel Street

Originally called *The Queens Head*, and occupying a small building and three cottages in what was then called Hog Lane. Had its first licence granted around 1820, when under the ownership of John Morris, and by 1876 was under lease to J. W. Green from the executors of James Cook of Luton.

The original house and cottages were demolished in 1896 when the lane was widened, which necessitated the destruction of most of the north side of the street. The rebuilt house was a very grand building for its time, being of three storeys featuring dormer windows on the upper floor.

During the 1960s this pub was the first in the town to feature a video jukebox, newly arrived from America. In the late 1970s it was converted from a typical two bar public house to a Berni Inn. It has been trading as *The Casa Bianca* and *The Italian Cafe* for a number of years and has been taken over this year (1994) by Chris Carroll, who also runs *The Kings Arms*, in partnership with ex-Luton Town footballer Mick Harford. They have converted the premises into a large 'Irish theme' public house by the name of *Rumours*.

It was in this pub, as *The Queens Head*, that the author remembers hearing news of J. F. Kennedy's assassination.

2   The Queens Hotel, 17 Chapel Street

A rather imposing building on the corner of Chapel Street and Victoria Street. The owner, Thomas Sworder, sold the premises in 1863 to the London and County Banking Company, who put in Ann Newman as tenant before 1876.

On the first floor was a large function room, much favoured by many local organisations for meetings. The room was a popular venue for wedding receptions, and was booked most weekends.

On the 12th October 1966, the Minister of Transport, Mrs Barbara Castle, gave the council the go-ahead to build the inner ring road. The property was bought by compulsory purchase order for £21,850, and on 2nd April 1967, the landlord William Fox and his wife Dora called 'last orders' for the final time; the building was then closed and demolished later in that year.

3   The Masons Arms, 56 Chapel Street

Already trading by 1842 when it was owned by Messrs. Burr and occupied by George Kitchener. The Burrs sold the pub to Frances Parsons of the St. Albans Brewery who in 1876 had Jubu Eaton as tenant. Two years later the brewery was sold to Adey and White, also of St. Albans.

The building was a small mid terrace house and it ceased trading as a pub around 1926. It still stands, but with a changed facade, and currently houses a motor repair shop and taxi firm. It stands between Regent Street and New Street.

4   The Kings Arms, 82 Chapel Street

Standing on the corner with Dumfries Street and has been trading since about 1855. It is most likely that it was opened as an unnamed beerhouse. Within several years of opening John King, brewer and cooper, owned the property. As well as selling his 'fine home-brewed ales on draught', he operated a 'take-away' service of casks in four and a half gallon barrels and upwards. His price list stated: 'XX at 1s. 0d. (5p). XXX at 1s. 2d. and Pale at 1s. 4d'. These prices were for quantities of one gallon.

It was most probably John King who named the house *The Kings Arms*. By 1872 the brewery and public house had been sold to Bennett's Brewery of Harpenden. In 1897 Bennett's public houses were sold by auction and it is likely that *The Kings Arms* came under the ownership of Mann, Crossman and Paulin at this time.

It has operated as a free house for many years, but is now owned by Marstons, as their only foothold in the town. It is run by Chris Carroll, an enterprising local man, who also owns *The Italian Cafe* further down Chapel Street.

There is an unusual fact about this house, it has two addresses, Chapel Street and Dumfries Street, and receives mail at each postal address.

5   The Albion Inn, 26 Ebenezer Street

In 1844 a parcel of land off Chapel Street was purchased by Jos Lawrence from William Townrow, a farmer, for £48. Lawrence, a bricklayer by trade, built six cottages on the land during 1846, and in 1860, Mr George Dukes converted three of the properties into a public house. He named his new pub *The Albion Inn*, it was also to be named, at various times, *The Albion Tavern* and *The Albion*. He wasn't new to the licenced house business as he already owned *The Salisbury Arms* in Wellington Street where his brother Jos Dukes was tenant. At the time that Jos Lawrence was building his properties, the Luton Rate Book for 1845 lists three unnamed beerhouses in the immediate area. One at Number 2 New Street, run by Henry Pedley, and two in Spring Place, operated by Richard Swain and Ann Caton. It is likely that George Dukes saw the potential business in the beer supply trade and that was the reason he converted three of his cottages into a public house. When George died, in 1879, his daughter, Kate, received both public houses in his will. By 1898, Jos owned *The Albion Inn*, selling the pub, five cottages and the land to Benjamin Bennett for £2,000.

The brewery concern Mann, Crossman and Paulin acquired the premises in 1938 and operated the site for the next twenty years. During 1958 the brewery wished to build a new public house on the site of the Biscot Mill and offered to surrender the licence of *The Albion Inn*, along with that of *The Welcome Stranger* in Duke Street, in order to gain a licence for the new pub at Biscot.

The house ceased trading on 24th November 1959 and was finally sold to Morris and Tear for £2,400 on 21st August 1964.

The building was demolished when the complete site, along with Ebenezer Street, was redeveloped for light industrial units.

6   The Regent's Arms, 11 Hastings Street

Built in 1842 on land owned by William Townrow and traded under the banner of Messrs. Burr until purchased by Thomas Sworder. It was originally called *The Cock and Magpie*.

The current tenants are John and Pat Timmons who have been in charge for seven months. They cater for a regular custom that is ninety-five per cent Irish, and is particularly busy at weekends. It is now being run by Whitbread Pub Partnerships.

7   Monty's, 23 Hastings Street

Built and opened at the same time as *The Cock and Magpie*. Benjamin Bennett was the first owner, but by 1876 Thomas Sworder was in control, having installed Thomas Cook as tenant.

For many years it was a Mann, Crossman and Paulin house before Watney Mann and was called *The Black Horse*. It now trades under the banner of Pubmaster.

8   The Two Brewers, 43 Dumfries Street

When first opened, midway through the last century, it went under the name of *The Standard*, later *The Royal Standard*.

The pub was in the news, when on 13th June 1978, the landlord of five years, Mr Maurice Whitney, was shot dead in the bar of his pub, allegedly by a woman friend.

A J. W. Green house of long standing it was closed in 1983 and reopened on Armistice day of that year as *The Two Brewers*, one of the first outlets to be owned and supplied by Banks and Taylor's Brewery at Shefford.

9   The Fountain, 152 Wellington Street

Originally owned by Henry Fowler of Woburn, and occupied, in 1876, by William Walker. A typical Victorian town centre public house, although somewhat larger than was usual. There were three stables, since demolished, at the rear as well as a large hall, regularly used for wedding receptions.

Mrs Rogers, who with her husband ran the pub from 1954 until their retirement in 1974, recalls that whenever the circus came to play a season at Stockwood Park, the stables were always booked to accommodate three bears.

It was also said, that a previous occupier would rent out the bottling shed, at the rear, for the sum of 2s. 6d. (12.5p) to the ladies of the street, for immoral purposes.

From 1988 until 1994 the landlord was John Kelly, recently moved to *The Phoenix*. It is currently (Nov. 1994) closed and offered for sale.

10   The Princess Alexandra, 50/52 Princess Street

Locally known as the Pretty Lady, it was purchased by Simpson's Brewery of Baldock in 1863 and occupied in 1876 by William Harrison.

1971 saw its closure and demolition, when the site was required for the building of the new magistrates court complex.

11   The Star and Garter, 35/37 Princess Street

This house stood on the opposite corner to *The Princess Alexandra*. This gave the customer a choice of two fine ales, Benskins and Greene King, for the bother of a ten metre walk. Slightly older than its neighbour, gaining its first licence in 1858, when it was owned by William Nash of Melksham, Wiltshire. It is not known who supplied the pub with beer in its early years, but it was later purchased by Benskins of Watford. It was closed and demolished in 1971 for the same reasons as the Pretty Lady.

12   The Duke of Edinburgh, 73 Stuart Street

The original inn of this name had stood on the corner of Stuart Street and Princess Street since at least 1855. The house was owned by Wells and Company of Biggleswade. The house was rebuilt in 1914 and given an imposing facade.

Most probably taken over by J. W. Green in 1947 when Mr and Mrs Fountain were the tenants. The last tenants, from 1955 until its closure and demolition in 1967, were Len and Edith Booth. They had moved from The Kings Head in Winchmore Hill, London. Reputed to have been the last public house in Luton to have retained its public bar spittoons. It was demolished to make way for the ring road development.

13   The Bedford Arms, 81 Stuart Street

Built and granted its first licence around 1850, and within a few years was already falling foul of the law. A meeting in Luton in September 1857 passed a resolution calling for magistrates to reduce the number of public houses in the town. Part of it read '. . . this rising town being very seriously compromised and corrupted by a torrent of vice and ungodliness, let loose on it not least through the operation of its lower class of public houses . . .'. As a result of this application, *The Bedford Arms*, by no means the worst public house in the town, had its licence temporarily suspended.

By 1876 it was owned and occupied by Francis K. Buckingham, who was possibly related to John Henry Buckingham, a brewer and maltster of Little Gaddesden.

Some time before 1897, it had been acquired by Thomas Sworder as it formed part of the sale of the business to J. W. Green.

Fell victim to the bulldozer in 1967 for the ring road development.

14   The Oddfellows Arms, 23 Dunstable Place

Previously called *The Oddfellows* when first trading around 1850, and owned by Benjamin Bennett of Harpenden. To the rear of the premises were stables and a smithy, although the entrance to the smithy was via an archway in Stuart Street.

The house was purchased from Bennett by Thomas Sworder in 1897, the year Sworder's business was in financial difficulties, and immediately before the sale to Green. The house was later sold to Mann, Crossman and Paulin.

Standing opposite the recently demolished police station, it was a popular haunt for off-duty police officers. During the late 1970s the pub featured as a magnet for the new wave (punk) aficionados.

During the eighties and early nineties, it was owned by Courage Group, but since 1993 has been a free house. Michael Hayes, a friendly Irishman and genial host has been in charge since 1991.

15   The Wellington, 58 Wellington Street

Built around 1824–25 when Wellington Street was first laid out as a private road, many of the houses being elegant homes for Luton's small band of professionals. It was operating as a brewhouse in 1845 when the tenant was John Abbott.

Owned from its early days by Thomas Sworder, it has undergone only slight renovation and alteration and remains, externally, much the same as the day it was built. Previous names have been *The Duke of Wellington* and *Wellington Arms*.

16   The King Edward the Seventh, 1 Peel Street

First mentioned in 1848 when called *the Bute Arms* and belonging to John Gray, a Luton brewer. One year later it was under the ownership of Messrs. Thomas and Robert Sworder. At the time of Green's acquisition of the Sworder empire, the pub was trading under the name of *The Volunteer Canteen*, being renamed *King Edward the Seventh* after the reign of the late King, 1901 to 1910, falling in line with the policy of public houses not being allowed to be named after a reigning monarch.

It was demolished in 1969.

The Queens Head, c. 1900. The house had been recently rebuilt at the time this photograph was taken.

map ref. 1

The Queens Head, c. 1960.   *(courtesy: Whitbread Archive)*
map ref. 1

The Queens Hotel. Standing empty and ready for demolition 1967.
map ref. 2   *(courtesy: Eric Meadows)*

Chapel Street, c. 1910. The building on the right was The Masons Arms. This is the only known photograph to show the public house. *(courtesy: Ken Cooper)*
map ref. 3

Chapel Street 1994. The centre building once housed The Masons Arms.
map ref. 3

map ref. 4   *The Kings Arms, c. 1953.(courtesy: Colin Glover)*

map ref. 4   *The Kings Arms 1994.*

The Regents Arms, c. 1953.
map ref. 6

(courtesy: Colin Glover)

The Black Horse, c. 1953.
map ref. 7

(courtesy: Colin Glover)

map ref. 5   *The Albion, c. 1953. Demolished 1958.*   *(courtesy: Colin Glover)*

map ref. 9   *The Fountain 1966.*   *(courtesy: Mrs Rogers)*

map ref. 8   *The Royal Standard, c. 1953.*   *(courtesy: Colin Glover)*

map ref. 8   *The Two Brewers 1994.*

The Princess Alexandra 1950. Demolished during 1971.   *(courtesy: Greene King)*
map ref. 10

The Princess Alexandra, c. 1953.   *(courtesy: Colin Glover)*
map ref. 10

The Star and Garter, c. 1930. Demolished in 1971.   *(courtesy: Benskins)*
map ref. 11

The Star and Garter, c. 1953.   *(courtesy: Colin Glover)*
map ref. 11

The Bedford Arms, c. 1966. Demolished 1967.   *(courtesy: Whitbread Archive)*
map ref. 13

The Bedford Arms, c. 1966.   *(courtesy: Whitbread Archive)*
map ref. 13

The Duke of Edinburgh, c. 1960. Demolished 1967.   *(courtesy: Stuart Goodyear)*
map ref. 12

map ref. 14   *The Oddfellows Arms 1994.*

The Wellington Arms, c. 1905.   (courtesy: Ken Cooper)
map ref. 15

map ref. 15   *The Wellington 1994.*

The King Edward the Seventh, c. 1960. Demolished 1969. (courtesy: Whitbread Archive)
map ref. 16

No. 63 Wellington Street. This building once housed The Lamb, formerly called The Wrestlers. It had closed by 1869 (see p. 144/5).

The building on the corner was once host to The Eagle public house, later The Yorkshire Hotel (see p. 144).

CASTLE STREET
and
WINDSOR STREET

This area featured in Luton's history long before any of the present buildings were thought of. In 1139 the foreign mercenary Robert de Waudari was just one of many soldiers hired by King Stephen to support his fight against the barons.

Waudari built a castle on the site of what is now occupied by the bus garage and the old Luton News building, now the Castle Street faculty of the University of Luton. The castle probably took the form of a wooden house mounted on an earth mound and surrounded by a deep dry ditch. It stood for fifteen years, before being pulled down in 1154. Evidence of the ditch was uncovered when the Luton News building was being excavated in 1963.

Seven centuries after the building of the castle, most of this area was developed with the building of typical mid to late Victorian terraced properties for the working classes. The public houses and beershops arrived at the same time, built to serve the indigenous population and not to capture the passing trade. None of these houses had stabling or coaching facilities, it being just too far out from the town centre to warrant such expense. Eight of the eleven public houses featured here still remain in business.

1 The Woolpack, 55 Castle Street

Built in 1867 as a private house and converted soon after into a public house, occupied at the outset by John Deeley. He and his wife remained in the pub until 7th August 1874, on which date the police were called to an incident where Deeley had attempted to murder his wife with a poker. He had inflicted grievous injuries to her head whilst he was in a drunken state. His wife survived and even pleaded for lenience for him when he was sent for trial. Although he had been in the town for twenty-eight years and had an unblemished character he was found guilty of attempted murder and sentenced to a long term in prison.

To replace John Deeley, Thomas Sworder installed William Crips as tenant. The house featured in the sale of Sworder's brewing empire to Green in 1897 and was still in business at the end of the Great War but closed soon afterwards.

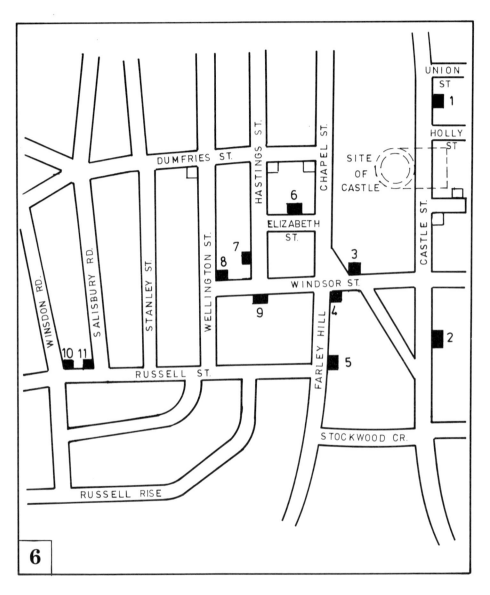

1 *The Woolpack*	6 *The Enterprise*	11 *The Stag*
2 *O'Shea's*	7 *The Butchers Arms*	12 *The Barn Owl*
3 *The Foresters Arms*	8 *The Salisbury Arms*	*(not on map)*
4 *The Farley Arms*	9 *The Royal Oak*	13 *The Parrot*
5 *The Compasses*	10 *Mac's Bar*	*(not on map)*

The building reverted back to a private dwelling before demolition in the 1960s to provide an extension to Barrett's garage and showroom.

2 O'Shea's, 115 Castle Street

The building dates from 1700 when it was one of a row of cottages. Joseph Isaac, of Harpenden, purchased them and they were converted into *The King Richard the Third* public house in 1846. Thirty years later it was occupied by Priscilla Yates and owned by James Mardall of Harpenden.

Extensive renovations took place in 1981, when the tenants were Phil and Des Perry. On re-opening night a free pint of beer was on offer to anyone using the pub whose name was Richard.

The house was renamed *The Tavern in the Town* and became a free house before the purchase and current name change during the early 1990s.

3 The Foresters Arms, 14 Windsor Street

Built around 1840 by Messrs. Burr, coming under the control of Sworder in 1857. Purchased by Green along with the rest of Sworder's business in 1897. The pub has undergone some external renovation, especially when first belonging to Whitbread.

The clientele has been mainly Irish for over thirty years, and on special occasions, such as St. Patrick's Day, the pub has been known to be extremely well attended and rather on the noisy side.

The pub is managed by Steve Magi for the owner, his uncle, local businessman Brendan Sherry.

4 The Farley Arms, 15 Windsor Street

One of the oldest public houses in this area, as it was trading in 1823. Francis Parsons owned and supplied the pub from his St. Albans brewery until 1885, when the brewery and its tied houses were sold to Adey and White, also of St. Albans.

J. W. Green purchased their brewery and houses in 1936, when this house was called *The Highlander*.

5 The Compasses, 11 Farley Hill

Already trading as a beerhouse in 1842 when owned and occupied by William Thorogood. At that time it went under the name of *The Mariners Compass*. By 1876 Francis Parsons of Princes Risborough was the owner and George Pollard tenant. It had already been renamed *The Compasses* and in 1912 the old pub was partially demolished and rebuilt on a larger scale than the old one.

It now comes under the banner of Charles Wells of Bedford.

6 The Enterprise, 20 Elizabeth Street

Has been trading on this site since 1865, when it was one of two public houses owned by James Cook of Luton, the other being *The Queens Head*. However, by 1876 the house was on lease to J. W. Green, from the executors of Cook's will.

From 1981 until 1984, Keith Gibbs, current tenant of *The Old English Gentleman*, was tenant here.

7 The Butchers Arms, 94 Hastings Street

At least 120 years old, this former beerhouse was owned, at the beginning, by Samuel Wright of Walkern. The first recorded transfer of licence was on 6th August 1879 but had been trading for several years before. It was sold to Simpson's Brewery of Baldock in 1924, at which time it was called *The Jolly Butchers*. Thirty years later, in 1954, the house came under the control of Greene King, when they purchased Simpson's brewing concern. The beerhouse licence was surrendered on 27th July 1966 and a full licence was granted for the sale of beers, wines and spirits.

8 The Salisbury Arms, 159 Wellington Street

Built in 1865 by George Dukes of Luton, who also owned *The Albion Inn* in Ebenezer Street. Joseph Dukes, the brother of George, was the tenant in 1876. Three years later, the daughter of George, Kate, owned both pubs.

Occupying the corner of Wellington Street and Windsor Street, the pub was extremely unlucky on 30th August 1940, when a flight of German bombers hit the Vauxhall factory during a daring daylight raid. The aircraft continued to drop bombs as they made their escape to the west. Along with many properties in New Town and Wilsden Road, then called Farley Avenue, the pub took a direct hit, completely demolishing it and resulting in the death of the landlady. Her grand-daughter was found alive among the rubble by Mr Archer, an ambulance driver called to the scene, and the young child was taken to Luton and Dunstable Hospital where she made a full recovery. The pub was never rebuilt, with the site being taken over by Sheaf's dairy for use as a delivery base. Modern housing now occupies the site.

There is no known photograph of this public house as it was before the raid.

9   The Royal Oak, 65 Windsor Street

Built in 1842 and operated as an unnamed beerhouse by George Pates. By 1850 the house was owned by Thomas Sworder and was given the name *The Royal Oak*. It was closed in 1962 with the licence transferring to *The Heron* on the Limbury Mead estate. The building still remains today, facing directly down the length of Hastings Street.

10   Mac's Bar, 80 Russell Street

Built in 1938 by Benskins to replace their public house and licence from *The Stag* just down the street. It was originally called *The Stags Head*, a name it was to keep until 1994 when it was given its present name. It occupies a large corner plot on the corner of Russell Street and Winsden Road.

11   The Stag, 76 Salisbury Road

The first recorded date of the licence for this house was December 1876 and it was almost certainly owned by Alfred Pryor of Hatfield, before his brewery was sold to Benskins Watford Brewery. The pub was closed in 1930 when the brewery wished to move the licence to a more opulent property that was built within a hundred metres of the old one.

The building was converted into a private dwelling which was to last for nearly another fifty years being being pulled down in 1986 to make way for modern housing.

12   The Barn Owl, Caddington Road

Opened in July 1977 on the edge of the small Leyhill Drive development. It helped serve the Farley Estate, which up till then had only *The Parrot* as a local.

It was decorated to resemble an old barn, with stuffed owls and assorted farm implements adorning the walls.

A good variety of food has always been available in the large bar and family room. It possesses a good spacious garden with pleasant rural views.

13   The Parrot, Whipperley Ring, Farley Hill

The building of the Farley Hill estate had begun in 1948, and this high density development did not have a local public house of its own until February 1960. It was built on a prominent position on Whipperley Ring and was a very welcome addition.

The name was transferred from the public house in New Town Street that had been demolished several years earlier.

Built and owned by Whitbread, it has enjoyed a thriving local trade since opening.

Castle Street, c. 1907. At the time of this photograph, The Woolpack occupied the taller of the two buildings in the centre. the inn sign is just visible.
map ref. 1

The Enterprise, c. 1953.   *(courtesy: Colin Glover)*
map ref. 6

map ref. 2   *The Richard the Third, c. 1953. (courtesy: Colin Glover)*

map ref. 2   *O'Shea's 1994.*

map ref. 3 *The Foresters Arms, c. 1953. (courtesy: Colin Glover)*

map ref. 3 *The Foresters Arms 1994.*

map ref. 4   *The Highlander, c. 1953.*   *(courtesy: Colin Glover)*

map ref. 4   *The Farley Arms 1994. Formerly The Highlander.*

map ref. 5   *The Compasses, c. 1953.*   *(courtesy: Colin Glover)*

map ref. 5   *The Compasses 1994.*

The Royal Oak 1953. Closed during 1968. *(courtesy: Colin Glover)*
map ref. 9

The Royal Oak, c. 1960. *(courtesy: Whitbread Archive)*
map ref. 9

map ref. 9   *This building once housed The Royal Oak.*

The Butchers Arms, c. 1950.   *(courtesy: Greene King)*
map ref. 7

The Stag, c. 1930. Closed 1938 and the building finally demolished 1986.
map ref. 11
(courtesy: Benskins)

The Stags Head, c. 1953. Built 1938.   *(courtesy: Colin Glover)*
map ref. 10

map ref. 10   *Mac's Bar 1994.*

map ref. 12   *The Barn Owl 1994.*

map ref. 13   *The Parrot 1994.*

LATIMER ROAD
and
NEW TOWN STREET

This area of the town was the first district to be developed separately, away from the original town centre, for the purpose of housing the growing working class community. Building began during the early Victorian years and the buildings were erected at an incredible rate. The standard and quality of many of the structures left much to be desired, with the building materials used ranging from good quality Luton bricks to plaster and lathe, and in some cases to wood and corrugated iron. The packed housing, built in some of the courts and lanes that ran off from the main streets, were the main ones to suffer from poor construction, consequently within a few years they were being classed as sub standard dwellings.

A report, in 1850, as to the health and living conditions of the people of Luton, paints a very damaging picture, especially among the working classes. Mr Kitt Tomson, surgeon, stated that 'He had attended 214 cases of fever during the years 1848 and 1849, which in Spring Place and neighbourhood assumed a very malignant character; the houses lately erected on the highest ground, particularly at New Town, were more affected that other parts, and where there was a want of drainage, the evil was most prevalent'.

Several rows of cottages poured out their drainage into open gutters. This refuse mixed with the contaminated liquid that was passed from the straw hat factories and bleaching houses and often drained into dumb wells and shafts. When these shafts were in close proximity to fresh water draw wells, the filth would seep through the lining and contaminate the drinking water. Complaints, as to the undrinkable condition of the water, were frequent. In this tightly packed community, the public houses and beershops thrived, possibly due to the ale being safer to drink than the water.

These premises tended to be at the heart of the working man's life and while very popular friendly establishments, because of the nature of the clientele they tended to be quite rough and ready, with many a fist fight and, on some occasions, near riots breaking out in or close by the pubs. The area abounded with tough colourful characters who lived their lives to the full, with much drinking and illegal street gambling.

By 1845, in New Town Street, there were six beerhouses listed, all unnamed. Some of these will have later been given names of pubs that are still there today, but undoubtedly some will have disappeared. There was a beerhouse called *The Garibaldi* at 45 Chase Street run by the Poulton family and one called *The Albert* in New Town Street, standing almost opposite *The Parrot*. This was owned, in 1842, by Messrs. Burr with George Tiplady as the tenant.

The Temperance Movement in Luton began to focus their attentions on the Magistrates Courts in an attempt to restrict the activities and licencing of existing and new beershops and public houses. A six hundred name petition was presented in 1858, which stated '. . . your memorialists feel assured that intemperance is the principal cause of misery, crime, prostitution and pauperism that exists in the town of Luton . . .'. This resulted in the Magistrates and Police curbing the activities of some of the more notorious licenced premises in the town. *The Robin Hood* and *The World's End*, which was operating as a beerhouse at that time, both had their licences suspended. This culling of public houses and their like would continue for many years, reaching a crescendo in 1869, when many of the worst offenders were closed down for ever. *The World's End* was one of these, as it was considered to be an habitual haunt of thieves and poachers. Within a year it reopened as an off-licence and remains as one to this day. An application for a beer licence was put before the Magistrates during September 1875 by Charles Barton of Chase Street. The police opposed the granting of a licence and it was duly refused; the reason for the refusal is not known. In the 1881 census returns for Chase Street, Charles Barton is listed as a shoemaker. If six years earlier, he had been practising his trade, maybe it was his intention to supply his customers with liquid refreshment in one room while he soled and heeled their shoes in the other!

Only two of the public houses featured here are no longer trading, a high remaining proportion compared to the heyday of the beershop, in the 1850s and 1860s.

1   The Globe, 26 Union Street

Built by Thomas Sworder in 1862 and has been in 'the family' of Green, Flowers and Whitbread ever since. There have been just twelve tenants in its 132 year history. G. Chamberlain was the first, from 1862 to 1869, followed by William Harris, 1869 to 1885. Eliza Graves, 1885 to 1903, Thomas Impey, 1903 to 1912, F. Taylor, 1912 to 1925, H. Frost 1925 to 1936, followed by his widow for three years. The war years found John White in occupation, he remaining until 1950. Over the next forty-two years, the house was occupied by just three tenants, Austin Walker until 1969, L. Milburn, 1969 to 1971, and the longest serving tenants, George and Annie Walker from 1971 to 1992. They left after celebrating their twenty-first anniversary in charge of the pub. It is now in the hands of Mr Brian Bluett, a very jovial likeable character.

2   The Mother Redcap, 80 Latimer Road

When this house was built in 1855, Latimer Road was called Langley Road, and was to retain that name until the 1940s.

The owners of this house, when new, was Simpson and Company of Baldock, the tenant being George Tennant. The pub was then called *The Red Cap*. This house had its licence suspended several times during the 1860s for offences ranging from keeping a disorderly house to selling drink after hours. The last offence would be considered trivial these days but during the temperance years, when many of the Magistrates were members of the movement, it was one more reason to come down with the heavy hand.

In 1935, the house was pulled down and rebuilt in the Tudor style, with its leaded windows and exposed exterior beams, a much prettier house now than the original, although the old pub had a distinctive rural feel to it. Perhaps the reason that many poachers were attracted to it!

It came under the control of Greene King in 1965, when they acquired the Baldock Brewery of Simpson's.

The origin of the name is rather obscure. It is said that public houses of this name could be named after Moll Cutpurse, the female highway robber of the 1650s, who had connections with Camden Town's *Mother Red Cap* pub, or there is possibly a link with Skelton's alewife Elynore Rummyng. Whichever is the explanation is unclear, but the name is a very common English public house title.

3   The Hibbert Arms, 35 Hibbert Street

The first recorded mention of a licence for this typical Victorian mid-terrace beerhouse was 29th June 1878. This was at the time when Hibbert Street was laid out, so it is most likely that the property was built as such. There is no record as to the first owners but it was purchased by Simpson's of Baldock in 1883.

A very attractive pub both inside and out, boasting a friendly atmosphere, and is now owned by Greene King.

4   The Phoenix, Kelvin Close

Built during the 1890s by Thomas Sworder before passing to Green's ownership. When built, this public house had its address as New Town Street, but in 1961 the flats in Kelvin Close were built, which necessitated the closing of this end of New Town Street.

From 1963 until his retirement in 1989, Mr Archie Ambridge was the

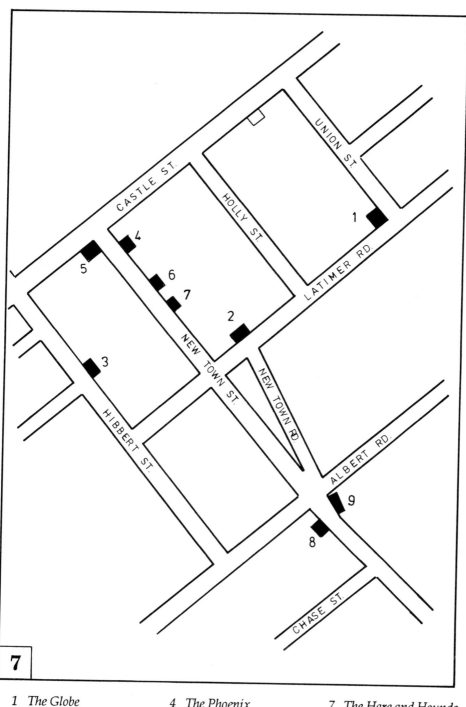

1   The Globe
2   The Mother Redcap
3   The Hibbert Arms
4   The Phoenix
5   The Vine
6   The Parrot
7   The Hare and Hounds
8   The Sugar Loaf
9   The Robin Hood

popular tenant of this house. He had seen naval service during the last war, his ship being captured in the Mediterranean. After spending some time on a German P.O.W. ship moored off the cost of South Africa, and then at Bremvorde P.O.W. camp in Germany, he finished his war years in Stalag 8B in Austria.

After the war, the family lived in Alfred Street and moved to Kelvin Close when their old home was demolished. The tenancy of *The Phoenix* was up for renewal within a short time of moving, and Archie recalls that he was urged to apply for the position. He was reluctant to work in a pub, but was successful in getting the licence and would remain there for the rest of his working life.

He recalls that the house was mainly patronised by the Irish community and busmen from the bus garage just fifty metres away. A room on the first floor was regularly hired out to the Metalworkers Union and to busmen for meetings.

Archie was instrumental in running a local football team playing under the pub's name, and, while trade was steady, it was never known as a crowded house.

During the last few years it has seen an upturn in trade and is now seeing its most profitable period since this end of New Town Street was closed.

5   The Vine, 89 Castle Street

This house was trading by 1842 when Alfred Pryor, of the Hatfield Brewery, was the owner and supplier and Sophia Ellard was the tenant. In 1920 the house was sold to Benskins, and then later purchased by J. W. Green. It has been extensively modernised and has been a free house for many years, with the widest choice of real ales in the town.

6   The Parrot, 23 New Town Street

William Ellord of Luton was the owner and occupier of this small house when it was built around 1845. It was later acquired by J. W. Green and was under the Flowers name when it was demolished in 1958 to provide a clearance area for the Kelvin Close flats. one of the last tenants, before demolition, was the brother-in-law of Diana Dors. It was her husband's family that had run *The Rabbit* public house in North Street during the 1950s.

The licence and name were later used for the new public house that was built in 1961 on Whipperley Ring.

7   The Hare and Hounds, 35 New Town Street

A typical mid Victorian beerhouse, having a comparatively short life span of about fifty years. There was a court conviction against the tenant, Charles Arnold, in 1875, for selling beer outside hours. His beers were supplied by Messrs. Fordham of Ashwell, Hertfordshire.

In 1909 it was kept by Mrs Chennels and by 1914, the last mention of the premises, it was occupied by W. Hibbocks. The building was demolished at the same time as its close neighbour *The Parrot*.

8   The Sugar Loaf, 98 New Town Street

The building was standing by 1842, and most probably was trading as a public house within a couple of years, if not from the outset. By the 1870s it was owned and occupied by Alexander Baxter of Luton. He was followed in 1878 by George Dickens who soon found himself before the courts, in April 1881, for permitting thieves and reputed thieves to assemble on his premises. The court was told that on several occasions the police had visited the premises and found certain persons there who were convicted thieves. The landlord was made aware as to the character of these persons but continued to allow them to gather in the pub. His line of defence was to state that he was a man of good reputation and that there was not one shred of evidence to say that the men were there with any criminal intent. The Bench agreed with him but decided to convict him anyway, but as they did not wish to come down on him too hard they decided not to endorse or suspend his licence but cautioned him as to his future conduct. This incident clearly shows the attitude of the pro-temperance lobby towards these 'evil dens of iniquity'.

During the last fifty years it has been a Mann, Crossman and Paulin house and is now run by Watney Mann.

The sign of the sugar loaf anciently represents, for those who couldn't read, the location of a grocer shop.

9   The Robin Hood, 81 New Town Street

Came onto the scene some ten years after *The Sugar Loaf*, about 1852, as it was trading as a licenced premises by 1855. Then it was under the guidance of Thomas Sworder. The house was regularly mentioned in the magistrates courts during the first dozen or so years of its existence due to the character of many of its customers, ranging from petty thieves and poachers to some notoriously violent men. It stood virtually on the doorstep of Chase Street, one of the worst areas for criminals and ne'er do wells, at least, according to the police and the courts. Illegal gambling was a common problem in this area and doubtless took place here with the police often called out to bring order to the proceedings. Several times during the 1860s the licence was suspended and the establishment can consider itself lucky not to have been one of the problem houses to have been closed down permanently.

The pub featured in the news again in April 1924 when Pc. Rhymes and his partner Pc. Wells came across a crowd of about sixty people, singing and shouting outside *The Robin Hood*. They were obviously under the influence of drink, and when asked to disperse quietly one of the men, an inhabitant of Chase Street, took a swing at one of the policemen. He was promptly arrested, whereupon the crowd was incited by another man to rescue the detainee, resulting in a large melée with cries of 'knock them down'. The crowd had now increased to over four hundred people and the situation for the two officers was looking very grim. Fortunately, on to the scene strode Sergeant Odell, a big powerful man known for his fearless approach to trouble. He was able, by his very presence and powers of persuasion, to disperse the crowd and send them on their way. The two prime movers in the near riot were arrested the next day at the pub, and despite one of them claiming that he wasn't at the scene and the other admitting that he had been 'very lively' on the night, they were both given prison sentences, one of twenty-eight days and the other receiving fourteen days and ten shillings (50p) fine.

Another story to bring some colour into the lives of the regulars, if indeed they needed any more, relates to a couple of Canadians who moved into the area and took lodgings above a cooked meat shop in New Town Street. One claimed to be a lumberjack and the other a cowboy from Alberta. They both frequented the pub and, being a boastful pair, it didn't take them long to fall foul of the regulars. The predictable outcome was that they both ended up in the Bute Hospital, very much the worst for wear. It is not known what became of them except that they were not seen in the pub again.

For all these incidents over the years the pub survived and thrived and during the late 1960s it was renovated and extended, by incorporating the adjacent shop into the pub. Mr Bill Granger was the tenant here from about 1969 until 1992. Since then it has been in the hands of Mr. P. Whitehurst. He is instrumental in raising a lot of money for charity; one of the latest schemes is arranging bungy jumps, the last taking place in the pub car park. The clientele is generally of a mixed age group, but on Thursday and Saturday evenings they feature live music, resulting in the pub being packed with many young customers. Around 1980 it was sold by Whitbread's to the Courage Brewery.

The pub sign is the most frequent of signs originating from country folklore and ballads.

map ref. 1   *The Globe, c. 1960.*

The Hibbert Arms, c. 1960.   *(courtesy: Greene King.)*
map ref. 3

The original Mother Redcap, c. 1935. Demolished 1935.(courtesy: Greene King)
map ref. 2

map ref. 2   *The Mother Redcap, c. 1965. Built 1935.*

map ref. 4   *The Phoenix, c. 1953.*   *(courtesy: Colin Glover)*

map ref. 4   *The Phoenix 1994.*

map ref. 5   *The Vine, c. 1960.*   *(courtesy: Whitbread Archive)*

map ref. 5   *The Vine 1994.*

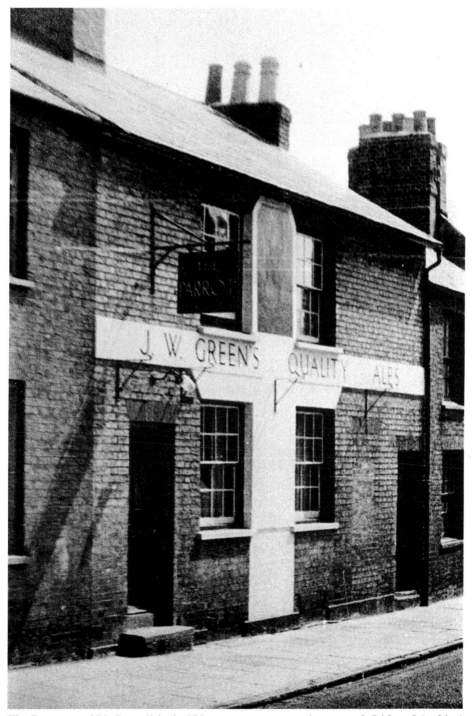

The Parrot, c. 1950. Demolished 1958.   *(courtesy: Whitbread Archive)*
map ref. 6

map ref. 8   *The Sugar Loaf, c. 1953.*   *(courtesy: Colin Glover)*

map ref. 8   *The Sugar Loaf 1994.*

map ref. 9   *The Robin Hood, c. 1953.*   *(courtesy: Colin Glover)*

map ref. 9   *The Robin Hood 1994.*

CHURCH STREET
and
BUTE STREET

The public houses featured in this section now surround the sprawling Arndale Centre, the oldest and most interesting pub being the only one to fall victim to the needs of the developers. They, in turn, provided a new public house when the centre was built, positioning it within fifty metres of the old inn.

The inns and taverns that were situated in Bute Street originally provided refreshment for the many hat trade workers that came into the town centre to work in this congested area, and also for the railway travellers using this new-fangled mode of transport. Three of the public houses here have a railway connection on their inn signs. Other than the pubs, this area also included many hat factories, hat warehouses and affiliated businesses, the swimming pool and public baths, the Grand Theatre, several cafes and later coffee bars, the first supermarkets in the town and the old covered market.

Unfortunately, the building of the Arndale had the effect of cutting Bute Street and Guildford Street off from the main town centre, and many of the publicans saw a downturn in trade, especially the trade to be expected from passing customers.

Several ancient inns, their exact positions not known, have plied their trade in Church Street. *The Barley Mow* was kept by Joseph Perren in 1853. Austin records that it was near the top of Church Street, on the north side. He also mentions *The Anchor* as standing in Church Street. From 1870 until around 1910, there was a beershop at 47 John Street kept by J. Gray, the building having since been demolished. Another beerhouse that stood in John Street, the exact location not known, was *The Grapes*, owned by McMullen and Sons between 1872 and 1876.

1   The Eight Bells, 43 Church Street

A tavern by this name had stood on the site since the fifteenth century. It had originally been called *The Five Bells*, the name being changed as the Church bell peal increased.

For generations, the Lucas Brother of Hitchin had owned the property, until 1921 when J. W. Green acquired their business and the brewery was closed down.

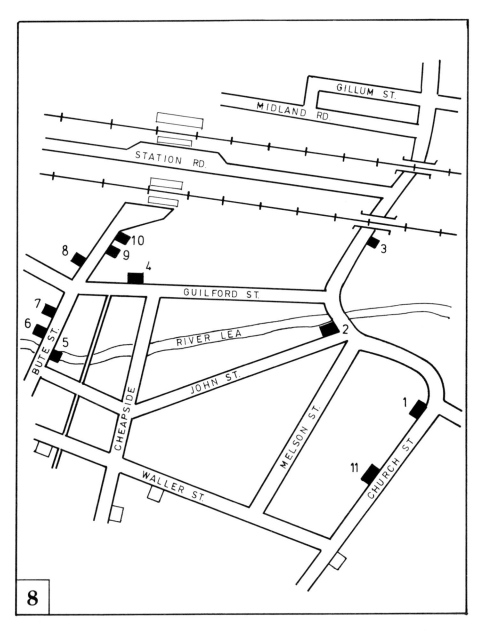

1	The Eight Bells	5	The British Queen	9	The Bridge Hotel
2	The Melson Arms	6	The Engine	10	The George the Second
3	Eddie's Bar	7	The Coopers Arms	11	The Traders Tavern
4	The Wheelwright's Arms	8	The Great Northern	12	The Shannon Hotel

The building was demolished in 1968, when the first stage of the Arndale development began.

2   The Melson Arms, 65 John Street

Built in 1856 by Thomas Sworder, one of the first tenants being J. G. Marshall. An unattractive pub from the outside and after the last war it did not have a very good reputation owing to a rough element that formed its clientele.

During the late 1960s, Whitbread decided to 'clean it up'. They invited Eddie and Brenda Feeney, a couple from Watford, to move into the pub and, with their help, make a go of it. Despite the damp in the cellars, (the river Lea ran directly under the house), dark and uninviting bars and very primitive licensee's accommodation, it was obvious to the Feeneys and the brewery that the house could be made very attractive.

The upstairs accommodation was modernised and redecorated, the cellars made free of water by diverting the river, and the two bars were upgraded by the addition of alterations and new furnishings. It was a successful move and the pub enjoyed a great increase in trade.

3   Eddie's Bar, 106 Church Street

Between 1858 and 1868, Luton gained two railway lines and two stations, both lines connecting with London. This led to a surge of traffic, horse drawn and pedestrian, to the Bute Street end of the town, and to the newly constructed Station Road. The house was opened in 1865 to avail itself of some of this potential business, much of the business being exploited by the 'ladies of the street' as there are many references to this house being the haunt of prostitutes and thieves. It was first named *The Midland Railway Tavern* and was owned by Francis Parsons of the St. Albans brewery.

The house has also been called *The Midland Tap* and *The Midland*.

4   The Wheelwright's Arms, 34 Guildford Street

One of several taverns originally titled to attract artisan custom.Built and opened around 1840 and belonging to Thomas Sworder. It followed the usual path of J. W. Green, Flowers and Whitbread until around 1985 when it was sold to Truman. After suffering from some problems with customers and gaining some adverse publicity, the renewal of its licence was refused in 1982 resulting in the premises closing and being put up for sale.

During the busy hat trade era, with many highloaded carts passing to and from the railway stations, it was not permitted for the inn to have a traditional hanging pub sign, so tools of the wheelwright's trade, together with a cart wheel, were mounted flush on the front facade of the inn. Recently, after yet another renovation, a J. W. Green illuminated sign has been mounted over the door. It was found in the loft space above the old outdoor toilets during 1992, after the pub was bought at auction by Mr L. Dalgarno who has installed his son as manager. He is proving an enthusiastic host with an avid interest in the history of his pub. It was he who found and re-installed the illuminated sign. A very welcome addition to this free house.

5   The British Queen, Bute Street

This tavern-cum-beerhouse stood opposite *The Engine*, directly above the river. With the story of Sweenie Todd in mind, its customers, nicknamed the tavern 'the tiddley wink the barber'. It was closed sometime before 1890, with its licence being transferred to *The Lea Bridge*.

6   The Engine, 45 Bute Street

Built in 1865 on the site of some old cottages and a blacksmith's yard. The original inn was much smaller than it is now, having been rebuilt by J. W. Green at the end of 1900.

Mr Thomas Thorne was landlord from September 28th 1898 until 1909. His yearly takings, which were £637 in 1899 rose to £1,426. 18s by 1904, and during his last year in charge were £1,778. 19s. A typical weekly takings in 1898 were £12. 5s, with Saturday the busiest and Monday the next most profitable. The difference in drinking habits then, compared to present days, is reflected in the takings book, painstakingly kept by Thomas Thorne. On Saturday 31st December 1899, the last day of the old century, the day's takings were only thirteen shillings (0.65p), lower than that on any day of the previous week. Imagine the pubs on the last day of this century, the customers will most probably be queuing to get in for the evening festivities from lunchtime onwards. Shortly before the rebuilding of the house, a typical week's takings were around £8, and during the month after reopening, they were up to £13. By September of that year they had increased to an average of £30.

The Engine was the second pub in the town to run a slate club, the first being *The Falcon*, and each year, at the start of his financial year, Thomas Thorne gave a slate club supper for his members.

Two notable dates when the day's takings showed an increase, were firstly on Saturday 16th January 1909 when Luton Town F. C. played at home to Millwall, in the first round of the F. A. Cup, in front of a seven thousand crowd. The takings trebled to £13. 14s. Most of the increase in trade on football days, doubtless arrived in Luton by train, with *The Engine* handily placed to serve them.

The second notable date was on Saturday 1st October 1910 when Luton's new free library opened its doors and takings soared to £25. 15s.

For the next fifty years after Thomas Thorne, the pub was kept by Frank Surtees. Each year he organised a harvest festival, the produce collected being donated to the old Bute Hospital. From 1986 until 1994 Derrick and Cathy Fletcher were popular tenants of this establishment.

This public house is one of the few remaining houses to retain the J. W. Green frosted windows between the bar and the street.

7   The Coopers Arms, 55 Bute Street

Its first licence was received in 1864 and it was purchased by Simpson and Company in 1875. The house has remained in the Simpson – Greene King organisation ever since.

This public house and *The Engine*, were both first hand witnesses to the worst peace time disaster to befall Luton. The building that stands between them, now the T.S.B., was Vyse's hat factory. In 1930 a serious fire broke out in the building during the working day, and although the rescue services were on hand, eight people perished, most of them women. It was said that over the years a build up of dust, cloth scraps and rubbish beneath the floorboards, on all floors, helped the flames accelerate through the building, cutting off escape for many of those who were to perish.

The licencees for the past nine years have been Frank and Eileen Sherry. Six years ago they had an extension added to the side of the house that used the space previously occupied by the side garage entrance.

The range of ales available, as usual from Greene King, is excellent in this friendly family public house.

8   The Great Northern, 63 Bute Street

There was a pub trading on this site around 1859 going under the name of *The Ship*. In 1876 it was owned by Messrs. Adey and White of the St. Albans Brewery with Donald McKillicon as the tenant. By 1879 the house had been renamed *The Great Northern*, most probably to be associated with the branch line of that company which had its station within a stone's throw of the pub. The line had been opened in 1860 so the change in name had been somewhat belated. It is now a grade 2 listed building constructed with Luton grey bricks, a much sought after commodity on the second hand market.

In 1921 the business of Adey and White was purchased by J. W. Green who then sold this house to Benskins. It remained in their hands until 1992, when the tenants, Mr and Mrs Cousins, who had been in the pub since 1985, became the new owners. They intend to extend the single bar to the rear during 1995, but will keep the Victorian green wall tiles in the bar, as well as the ceiling gas lights. This must be the only public house in the town to retain many of its original fittings.

A warm welcome is guaranteed in this friendly free house.

9   The Bridge Hotel, 66 Bute Street

This hotel occupied part of a building with late eighteenth century origins for about forty years. It is now trading as a restaurant.

10   The George the Second, 68 Bute Street

This house was in business by 1862, and within ten years was purchased by Simpson and Company. The sign commemorates the son of George the First, Elector of Hanover, who ascended the throne in 1714, without being able to speak English.

The house was extensively refurnished and updated during the 1980s, and is well respected for its choice of fine ales. The current tenants are Mr and Mrs Abraham, who have been there for three years. Live music is a feature of Thursday and Saturday evenings when the pub is very busy with a young trade.

11   The Traders Tavern, Church Street

Opened by Whitbread on April 20th 1972, soon after the first phase of the Arndale development opened. At first it was called *The Student Prince* and featured three levels. The ground floor level, called the College bar, was modelled on a small German bier keller. The next level, connected by an internal stairway, was a restaurant, specialising in German and English food. Another stairway connected to the Market Bar, which was also accessible from the mall and market. The whole place had a Bavarian theme.

Changes have taken place, so that now the ground floor is a club, with the bar and restaurant separated.

Before its latest name change it has also been called *The Baron of Beef* and *The Elephant and Tassel*.

12   The Shannon Hotel, Guildford Street

Opened in 1992 and occupies part of the same building as *The Great Northern*. Has a distinctive Irish flavour in this attractive addition to Luton's hotels.

map ref. 1   *The Eight Bells, c. 1955. Demolished 1968.*   *(courtesy: Whitbread Archive)*

map ref. 2   *The Melson Arms, c. 1953.*   *(courtesy: Colin Glover)*

map ref. 3   *The Midland, c. 1953.*   *(courtesy: Colin Glover)*

map ref. 3   *Eddie's Bar 1994.*

map ref. 4   *The Wheelwrights Arms, c. 1953.*   *(courtesy: Colin Glover)*

map ref. 4   *The Wheelwrights Arms, c. 1962.*   *(courtesy: Whitbread Archive)*

The Engine, c. 1950.   *(courtesy: Whitbread Archive)*
map ref. 6

The Coopers Arms, c. 1948.   *(courtesy: Greene King)*
map ref. 7

The Great Northern, c. 1930.   *(courtesy: Benskins)*
map ref. 8

The George The Second, c. 1955.
map ref. 10

(courtesy: Greene King)

map ref. 11   *The Traders Tavern 1994.*

map ref. 12   *The Shannon Hotel 1994.*

HIGH TOWN

The area now known as High Town, which for the purposes of this section covers the ground from North Street to Hitchin Road, had its earliest mentions during the latter half of the eighteenth century. Then, it was part of one of the main fields of the township of Luton, and called Burge or Bridge Field.

By 1815 the large Burge Field had become mainly privately owned smaller fields, some enclosed by hedges. Part of the field had been called Windmill Hill, after the post-windmill, belonging to Joshua Everitt, which had stood in the vicinity of the junction of High Town Road and Midland Road. It had long since disappeared, having apparently blown down in a gale during the middle 1700s.

The first building is reputed to have been a Baptist meeting house, built with bricks, taken from the old meeting house on Park Street, and transported on the back of a donkey up to Windmill Hill. The house was dubbed 'Donkey Hall', apparently in contrast to Coney Hall, or it might be a reference to the steepness of the hill, or the donkey haul. As further building took place, the area became known as Donkey Hall.

Between the building of the first houses, in 1815 and 1842, the lower half of High Town, from Burr Street, yet to be laid out, was basically completed. The area known as Coney Hall, which was around the North Street and Bedford Road junction, had also started to see the first development.

It must be remembered that in 1842 and before the arrival of the railways, High Town reached down as far as Love Lane, an ancient road that lay approximately where Station Road now runs. The road, or track, then forded the river and entered the town by way of Barbers Lane.

Considering how few buildings and inhabitants there were, compared to just twenty years later, the people of High Town were well served by beerhouses and public houses. By 1842 there were five public houses and several beerhouses.

The first mention of pubs occurs in the 1834 Rate Book, when it was recorded that there was *The Windmill, The Bricklayers Arms, The George the Fourth* and *The Waggon and Horses*. These were followed within ten years by *The Sun Inn* and *The White Horse*.

It is possible that *The Bricklayers Arms* was trading before 1834, as the land had been purchased by Joseph Gutteridge from the Browns in 1820, and that by 1824 he had built a house on the land. Whether it was operating as a licenced premises from the start is not recorded. In 1845 there was an unnamed beerhouse standing four properties above *The Bricklayers Arms*. It was being run by William Barber.

The Windmill stood next door to the present *Blockers Arms* on the side away from the town. It was owned and occupied by William Cotchins, and is reputed to have been built in Windmill Field.

The George the Fourth, owned by William Honeydon, was to have its name changed to *The Mitre*.

The Waggon and Horses is known to have been in the lower end of Hitchin Road, opposite and slightly above the *The Old English Gentleman*. The site is now occupied by Powdrill's furniture repository building. It was owned by Benjamin Bennett of Harpenden and was to close around 1854.

The Sun Inn, owned by Richard Brown, was positioned on the corner of Back Street and Love Lane with *The White Horse* its neighbour in Love Lane.

A beerhouse by the name of *The Cricketers* operated in High Town Road during the final two decades of the last century. It stood on the same side as *The Painters Arms* and was positioned opposite the top of Brunswick Street.

By 1850 345 houses had been built in High Town, and an inspector to the General Board of Health commented that some of the property, especially in Burr Street which was only just seven years old, were in a 'filthy state', and that the occupants were 'seldom without fever, particularly at the lower end where the slaughter house is situated'. Most of these properties were to remain occupied for another hundred years, until they became the first buildings, on a large scale, to be demolished in the town.

The population of High Town was then around 1,800, with only 800 people over the age of twenty. As the male population totalled forty-five per cent of this figure, then it is clear that the drinking men were well catered for. These men were inevitably from the poor and working classes, with a few of the poorer men of the district supplementing their meagre wages with the proceeds of petty crimes such as poaching, theft and the dealing in stolen property. Many of the deals and plans were struck and made in the local beerhouse rather than the public house, due to the drink generally being cheaper, sometimes in quality as well as in price. Very few Lutonians viewed the crime of poaching as a serious offence but the same can not be said of the Magistrates Court. Invariably, these were presided over by country gentry and the clergy with very few representatives from the urban area itself. The decisions and sentences handed down therefore represented rural Bedfordshire's values, not Luton's.

By 1851, there were two beerhouses trading in York Street, *The Duke of York,* owned by Thomas Sworder, and *The Harp.* In Duke Street there was a particularly notorious beerhouse called *The Lord Nelson,* also a Thomas

Sworder house. This establishment frequently fell foul of the law with licence offences and the fact that the criminal fraternity of High Town tended to gather there. In August 1859, David Stratton, landlord, was charged with 'permitting drunkenness and encouraging disorderly and evil-disposed persons to assemble in his house'. The police sergeant sent to arrest a man, accused of assaulting his wife, found him in *The Lord Nelson* at noon with other notorious local men, all of whom were drunk and disorderly. A fracas ensued leading to one of the men, John Day, who was later described in court as 'one of the worst characters in the town', being fined and bound over to keep the peace. The court was told that the establishment kept by Stratton 'is a very bad one, a regular resort for thieves, prostitutes and other bad characters; one of the worst houses in Luton'. The reputation of this house did not imply that all the beerhouses in the area were the same. Most were run by honest men striving to provide a much needed service and make an honest living.

Apart from *The Fortune of War*, later *The Britannia*, there were two other beerhouses in Burr Street. Both unnamed, one was getting mention as early as 1845, the other, owned by a Mr Gregory with a Mr Aldridge as tenant, was mentioned during 1869. At this time, one of Burr Street's beerhouses was trading as *The Black Boy*, where the landlord was 'a bad character', and along with *The Fortune of War* both had periods of licence suspenson. By 1876, *The Black Boy* had closed for good, as had several other beerhouses, including *The Tiger*, the whereabouts of which are uncertain.

In 1867, a murder at Stopsley, committed by three High Town men, shocked the people of Luton. William Worsley of Duke Street, Levi Welch of Burr Street and James Day, aged twenty-two, of Back Street, all said to be notorious poachers, had spent a heavy night drinking in *The King Harry* and later at *The Royal Oak*, Round Green. They met William Bradbury, a gamekeeper on the Putteridge Estate, who had himself been drinking in *The Old English Gentleman*, and after an altercation of some kind, murdered him. At their trial the older men claimed that Day had not been involved and he was acquitted. Welch was imprisoned, later to be given a free pardon, and Worsley was hanged at Bedford the following year.

It is interesting to note that in 1874, seven years after the murder, applications for a drinks licence to sell on the premises were received at the licencing sessions from a James Day for *The Blockers Arms* and an unnamed beerhouse at number 6 Taylor Street. Whether this applicant was the same man acquitted in the murder case is not known as there was a large family of Days in the area at that time. The licences were granted, as well as licences for *The Dudley Arms* in Dudley Street, which was applying for a renewal after having been suspended some years earlier, *The Duke of Cambridge* in Duke Street, kept by Henry Andrews and owned by the Redbourn Brewery, and *The Royal Oxford Arms* beerhouse in Hitchin Road, where the licence had been suspended, for contravening the Licencing Act, at least twice, in 1859 and 1869.

The Duke of Cambridge was one of the beerhouses that was finally refused a licence to sell beer for consumption on the premises and was closed down, only to reopen within a year as an off-licence. It served in this capacity until falling victim to the bulldozer in the 1960s.

In 1862, when the Midland Railway Company built their own line through Luton, they wanted to build a station alongside that of the Great Northern line, so they purchased enough land to build it and some railway sidings. This resulted in Love Lane and the lower part of High Town being demolished, a total of ninety properties being lost. An extensive excavation took place to provide a level site for the station, and this resulted in the demolition of both *The Sun Inn* and *White Horse*. The only building remaining from the old bottom end of High Town is the station master's house, which can be seen today alongside the footbridge.

Midland Road was laid out at this time, being called at first New Love Lane. *The George the Fourth*, then called *The Mitre*, was at the extreme bottom end of High Town Road.

About this time there were seven other unnamed beerhouses in High Town Road, the location of six of them is unclear, but one at 77 High Town Road, next door to the original *Painters Arms*, was kept by Thomas Huckle and was to remain in business for one year only, 1873. There were also beerhouses, at various times, in Brunswick Street and Windmill Street.

The heyday of the public house trade in High Town was in 1901, when there were eighteen public houses and sixteen beershops in this area, about half the total number of beershops in the whole of the town.

1   The Old English Gentleman, 17 Hitchin Road

Built around 1845, its first tenant was Thomas Ginn, with Edward Angell following him. It was owned by Thomas Sworder, and once had stables at the rear to cater for the coach trade on the Hitchin Road.

The pub found new owners in the early 1990s in the form of Inn Business, and a new landlord, Mr Keith Gibbs, took over in 1994. He had previously been licensee at *The Bitter End* and also *The Enterprise*.

2   The King Harry, 59 Hitchin Road

Opened in the late 1850s under the name *King Henry the Eighth* and by 1869 had its licence suspended when trading as *The Kings Head*. It was renamed *Harry the Eighth* by 1876, when it was under the ownership of Thomas Sworder and occupied by Edward Fox.

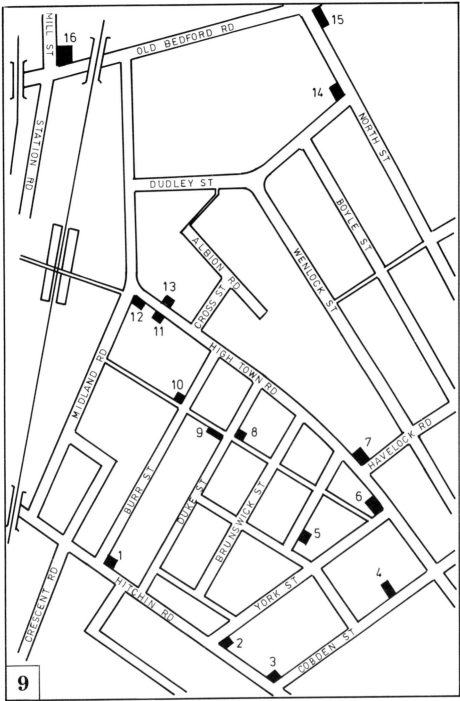

9

1	The Old English Gentleman	
2	The King Harry	
3	Maggie's	
4	The Burton Arms	
5	The Yorkshire Grey	
6	The Freeholder	
7	The Painters Arms	
8	The Green Man	
9	The Welcome Stranger	
10	The Britannia	
11	The Bricklayers Arms	
12	The Railway Tavern	
13	The Blockers Arms	
14	The North Star	
15	The Wabbit	
16	Taboo	
17	The Gardners Call (not on map)	

215

By the time that Sworder's business was sold to Green in 1897, it had been renamed *The King Harry*, a name it was to keep until its closure.

'Last orders' were called for the final time on 22nd September 1964 and the pub had a special customer on that night. The guest was Mrs Alice Wood, a ninety year old widow who lived opposite the pub at 74 Hitchin Road. For seventy years, she had gone to the pub for a pint of beer in a jug, and had carried it home to drink. The tenant, Mr John Packman, in recognition of this feat, invited Mrs Wood in on the last evening, sat her down at a table and treated her to a drink. This was the first and last time she took a drink in the pub itself. Her first memories of *The King Harry* were as a six year old, in 1880, when she would cross the road and fetch a jug of beer for her father.

The house was closed to make way for a road widening scheme. The road was eventually widened, resulting in the demolition of Mrs Wood's house, but the pub remained, and is still in use today as business premises.

Mr Packman took over the tenancy of the new *King Harry* in Fermore Crescent, the day after his pub closed.

3   Maggie's, 85 Hitchin Road

When opened around 1874 it was called *The New Inn* and was owned by Eleanor Lucy Leigh of Luton Hoo. It was acquired by Thomas Sworder during the 1890s. After being renamed *The Harrow* it traded under the guidance of Green, Flowers and Whitbread before becoming a free house in the early 1990s.

4   The Burton Arms, 29 Cobden Street

Built and granted its first licence in 1962 under the ownership of John Dear of Baldock. He was listed as a brewery clerk in 1853 for the Baldock Brewery. It was purchased by J. W. Green early this century and traded until its demolition in 1973 during the High Town redevelopment program.

5   The Yorkshire Grey, 8–10 Welbeck Road

Opened around 1855 by Thomas Sworder but within ten years had been sold to Samuel Wright of Walkern. It remained in Wright's hands until 1924 when the brewery ceased beer production. On 28th February 1924, Herbert Wright estimated the value of the property at £2,855. 7s. 10d, as there had been a consistent drop in trade during the last two years. It was noted that eighty-four less barrels of beer and thirty-six gallons less spirit were sold in 1923 compared to 1921. Simpson's Baldock brewery and Benjamin Bennett of Harpenden, who also had a brewery in Dunstable, were in the market for the property, with Simpson's being the successful buyers.

It was to remain trading for another thirty-five years before it was one of the first public houses in the area to be demolished in 1959. The licence was transferred to *The Hansom Cab* in April 1958.

6 The Freeholder, 45 York Street

Built around 1855 by Thomas Sworder and already having a licence suspension before the decade was out for licencing offences. Within a year a renewal application was successful and it has traded ever since. The tenants from 1972 until 1978 were Derrick and Cathy Fletcher. Currently owned by Whitbread's.

7 The Painters Arms, 79 High Town Road

John Steed of Baldock was the original owner and supplier of this property. It was a much different building when first opened in 1865. Then it was a small corner pub with no outstanding features. During the 1890s the house was sold to Pryor, Reid and Company.

In 1913 the old house was pulled down and the Edwardian style pub, that now stands, was built. It featured a series of bars, including a delightful 'snug' surrounding a central servery. The bars retain almost all their original features, including the polished oak joinery, etched cut glass and glazed tile dados, with more than a hint of Art Nouveau. In 1920, the business of Pryor, Reid and Company was sold to Benskin's, in whose hands it still remains.

Some fame was attached to Sylvia Hawkes, the step-daughter of Frank Swainson, who was tenant during the 1930s. She was remembered for her youthful beauty and bearing. After spending her childhood in the pub, she married the Earl of Shaftesbury's heir, Lord Ashley, after which she proceeded to break up the romance of Mary Pickford and Douglas Fairbanks, whom she later married. When this failed, she was married in turn to Lord Stanley of Alderley, Clark Gable and finally Prince Djordgadzi. She died in 1977 aged seventy-three.

8 The Green Man, 52 Duke Street

Built during the second phase of the High Town development around 1865, by which time Duke Street and Back Street were already densely populated. The buildings in this vicinity were described, at the time, as being closely packed together, with dumb wells and open waste channels on the surface. There was no underground drainage, with the gutters nearly on the level of the living rooms. To every six houses there was only one privy, most of them in a filthy condition.

This was the type of neighbourhood that the newly opened public house was to serve. Owned by George Sole of Stopsley when built, with William Worboys as publican. In 1930 the Bedford brewers Charles Wells took over the house and have kept it since.

In 1935 Jesse William Hannell, the father of Josie Fensom, Luton's Mayoress in 1993–4, took over from a Mr Mare and was to run it throughout the war years until 1951. Josie recalls that when her father and mother, Connie, took over as the youngest tenants in Luton, the house was a typical back street Victorian pub, very small and a little seedy. Nevertheless, Connie remembers her time in the pub as the happiest days of her life.

Within a couple of years the brewers decided to invest some capital in the building and carry out a rebuilding exercise. The work began in 1938, and during the following year it was completely restructured while the family were still in residence. After many trials and tribulations, while the building was knocked down and rebuilt around them, it reopened just as the war began. It featured a large smoke room, lounge and a jug and bottle.

Josie and her mother remember many characters and escapades during their time there, many of them during wartime. It was a popular haunt with many of the American soldiers billeted in and around the town and their nights spent drinking in the pub would sometimes end with a fighting finish. Evenings such as these were not unusual to *The Green Man*, nor to many of the public houses that catered for military personnel in wartime. The soldiers, especially the American GI's, tended to have money to spend and, combined with the thought that they might soon be going overseas, wished to enjoy themselves and would occasionally drink to excess. The drink, along with the racial tension that was present at that time in the American forces, would sometimes trigger off internal feuds which in turn would lead to trouble both inside and outside the premises, no doubt to the amusement of the local youngsters. Maybe as a result of this type of trouble, the short supply of beer glasses during the war led to Mr Hannell selling his beer in jam jars, the beer having been supplied by J. W. Green when Charles Wells could not meet the demand due to shortages of the raw materials and the rationing of fuel for the motorised drays.

Mrs Fensom's father was a well liked man, a character and a bit of a rogue, not averse to obtaining luxuries and necessities from the Americans on the 'black market'. The family rarely went without fresh fruit and meat, both in short supply and on ration, and Josie often remembers going to sleep, as a young girl, with a side of pork or hands of bananas secreted beneath her bed.

In 1946 she clearly remembers a handsome blue-eyed gentlemen using the pub several times while he was in the process of wooing a young lady from the Richmond Hill area. This young lady can consider herself very lucky that the budding romance was nipped in the bud due to the man getting himself arrested. It transpired that he was Neville Heath, the ex-RAF officer, who had butchered and murdered two ladies, one in London and the other in Bournemouth. These vicious sadistic attacks defy description and it can only be conjecture if he had the same designs on the Luton girl. He was hanged at Pentonville prison on 26 October 1946.

During his time in the pub Mr Hannell employed two men who were also well known in the area, Percy Crawley, from Back Street, acted as barman and George Morgan as his pot-man.

9   The Welcome Stranger, 61 Duke Street

Opened in 1866, and traded for ninety-two years as a beerhouse and cheap lodging house. It was owned during its early years by John Langridge of Dunstable, but it remains unknown as to the identity of the supplying brewery.

Mr Gutteridge of Stopsley recalls that in the 1930s it was kept by Mr A. Puddephatt, a short man of five feet tall and extremely fat. He took to wearing a straw boater all year round.

On the ground floor was the bar and rooms for the lodgers, and when a customer left the bar to visit the toilets he had to pass down a short hall that ran past the accommodation. Very often the lodgers could be seen cooking their meals on an old dirty stove. Most of the overnight customers worked in the building trade and would be charged ten pence (4p) per night for a bed.

During the last war the house was kept by Carrie Smith, a lady from Southend, and she is best remembered for her exceedingly loud pet parrot and for the fact that every Saturday evening she provided winkles and shrimps for her regulars.

It was closed in 1957, when the owners, Mann, Crossman and Paulin, gave up the licence, along with that of *The Albion* in Ebenezer Street, so that they could build a new public house in Biscot Road and gain one new licence for the loss of two. The building was demolished during the same year.

10   The Britannia, 63 Burr Street

A Thomas Sworder property from its first days of business during the late 1840s. It traded under the name *The Fortune of War* until 1870 when it was renamed *The Britannia* and remained so for the rest of its active life.

The house, standing in the midst of one of the poorest districts of High Town, gained a reputation as a hard, rough public house, certainly to people from outside the area, while no doubt to the indigenous population, it would have been as friendly as a beacon in the night. During the first twenty years of trading this establishment frequently incurred the wrath of the Magistrates and Licencing Sessions due, in most part, to the activities of its clientele, many of which, in the opinion of the Bench, were petty criminals.

The last tenants, before its closure and demolition in 1957, were Mr and Mrs Harris. They moved on to manage *The Brickmakers Arms* at Stopsley, while the name was used for a public house that was built three years later in Biscot Road.

11   The Bricklayers Arms, 16–18 High Town Road

Along with *The Windmill*, which stood almost opposite, it was one of the earliest public houses in High Town. It stands on land that was, in 1707, owned by the Crawleys. It came into the hands of Joseph Gutteridge in 1820, and within two years he had erected the original buildings. By 1834 the pub was trading as *The Bricklayers Arms*. Since 1842 the house came under the ownership of Messrs. Burr, who installed Thomas Peck as tenant. The property passed through the hands of Sworder, Green, Flowers and then Whitbread.

During the late 1970s it closed and reopened as a licenced pool hall, going by the name of *The Bronx*, and is now run, in conjunction with Whitbread, by B. and T. of the Shefford Brewery, under its original name.

12   The Railway Tavern, 2 High Town

This old public house was open for business in 1834 and by 1842 was owned by Alfred Pryor of Hatfield, with the tenant being John Mackerneys. The premises began life as three small cottages but were quickly converted into the building that stands today, its age making it one of the more important buildings in High Town. From its original position, one hundred metres up from the bottom of the road, it now occupies the prime site of being the first house that most visitors become aware of when crossing the railway bridge into the area. The building, of course, has't moved but the houses standing below it were demolished to make way for the excavation of the railway station.

It holds the dubious distinction of having the most name changes of all of Luton's pubs. From its construction to the present day it has had seven names. During the first sixteen years it was called *The George the Fourth, William the Fourth* and *The Three Jolly Butchers*. For a time it was named *The Mitre*, but after the building of the railway in 1867, the fact was celebrated by another name change to *The Railway Inn*. It retained this name until about 1960 when it reverted back to *The Mitre*, only to have its seventh and current name of *The Railway Tavern* during the 1980s. After the coming of the railways the house, unfortunately, gained a reputation as the haunt of prostitutes, no doubt seeking to increase trade from the new age travellers, and the landlord was frequently before the Magistrates in connection with the 'oldest profession'.

It is now owned by Inn Business and in June 1994 re-opened after being closed for a number of months. The licensee is Mrs Watts.

13   The Blockers Arms, 5 High Town Road

Originally a beerhouse, built almost on the site of the old *Windmill* which was High Town's first licenced public house. At first it was owned by the Lucas Brothers of Hitchin and tenanted by Albert Andrews. During the 1850s and 1860s, along with *The Lord Nelson, The Black Boy* and *The Fortune of War*, this establishment was among the worst licenced premises in the whole of High Town, if not in Luton. The landlord was frequently charged with keeping a disorderly house and allowing thieves and poachers to frequent his establishment. There were several licence suspensions but after renewal applications it always reopened for business. It was to be another one hundred and twenty years before the unruly behaviour of its clientele was to be instrumental in closing the doors to the paying public.

In 1921 the Hitchin brewery and its tied houses were purchased by J. W. Green, who then closed the brewery but retained the pubs.

During the late 1970s and early 1980s, the pub became a mecca for some of the undesirable elements of Luton society, it being reported that the pub was used by drug peddlers, with the result that there was much trouble with fights and under-age drinking. The renewal of the licence was first refused in 1986 with the house closing soon after. It was opened again for a short time but after more troubles it closed around 1990 and remains closed with its future uncertain.

14   The North Star, 22 North Street

Not exactly considered to be in High Town but it still served that population, being only a few minutes' walk away. It was granted its first licence in 1868 when owned by Mary Hart of Luton. Purchased by Green early this century and remaining a cosy corner pub until demolition in 1969.

15   The Wabbit, 46 Old Bedford Road

The original name, *The Rabbit*, was derived from the name of this area, Coney Hall, and was trading as a public house by 1845 for Thomas Sworder. John Ireland is believed to have been the first tenant. It is generally considered that the pub was built on the site of the eighteenth century Coney Hall. A coney was an early name for a rabbit. The house underwent a rebuild in 1908 but there is no known photograph of the original building.

During the afternoon before the peace day riots in 1919, the pub was crowded with would be rioters, no doubt feeding their thirst and anger which would explode in scenes of violence and arson later in the day.

There is a film industry connection with the pub, in that the late Diana Dors was married to David Hamilton, the son of Stanley Gittins who was tenant during the 1950s. It is reputed that she would often help pull pints behind the bar, a rare, glamorous treat for the inhabitants of North Street.

In 1978, the brewers Truman spent £30,000 in giving the pub a top to bottom face lift, which included knocking the two original bars into one. The name was changed to the present one in 1983, maybe to appear more up to date and trendy with a connection to the Warner Brothers' Looney Toons character.

16   Taboo, 1 Mill Street

This house was called *The Royal Hotel* and was in existence before the first train chugged past in 1860, providing stabling for the railway company's horses.

Over eight hundred years ago, it was by the Royal yard in Mill Street that there stood a mill which found mention in the Domesday Book.

Just before the last war the hotel was entirely reconstructed into its present condition. During the 1950s and the 1960s it was an up-market public house before the advent of live pub music and discos. It closed as a public house around 1982 to reopen as a club-disco under the name *Ronnell's*. Since then, there have been several internal structural alterations with a recent name change and it is now operated as a fun-pub with a disco, *Mirage*, incorporated on the premises.

17   The Gardeners Call, 151 High Town Road

Opened in 1869 by Simpson's Brewery of Baldock and was trading as an unnamed beerhouse in 1876 under the tenancy of James Nicholes. In September 1910, Mr Charles Taylor gave up his job in engineering and took over the pub for the Baldock company. He was thirty years old when he started and, apart from two and a half years spent in Salonika with the Royal Garrison Artillery during the Great War, he was to remain in the pub for forty-seven years until ill health forced his retirement in 1957. He was a keen amateur boxer and retained his interest in the sport all his life. When aged thirteen he had run away from home to join Thurston's travelling fair and gained his skills in the boxing booths. These skills he was later to put on view during amateur bouts at the Plait Halls in Luton.

When Charles first arrived at the house beer was 2d (1p) for a pint, with a screw of tobacco 1d. and a clay pipe thrown in for free. The premises were still operating as a beerhouse and it was in 1938 before a wine licence was acquired by Charles Taylor, at his own expense, with his supplies of wine coming from the Aylesbury Wine Company. It was another eight years before a full licence, to sell spirits as well, was granted and the pub could then compete on equal terms with other premises in the locality.

Mrs Alma Jeynes, daughter of Charles Taylor, recalls that whenever any alterations were planned for the building, like the 1937 living quarter extension, Miss Simpson, a director of the brewery, would personally come over from Baldock to view any plans. It is possible that it was Mrs E. P. Shaw-Hellier, Chairman of the brewery and grand-daughter of Joseph Simpson, who was operating a 'hands-on' system of management, a style much favoured by Simpson's Brewery Ltd.

It came under Greene King's ownership in 1954 when they purchased the Simpson Brewery.

map ref. 1   *The Old English Gentleman, c. 1953.*   *(courtesy: Colin Glover)*

map ref. 1   *The Old English Gentleman 1994.*

map ref. 2   *The King Harry, c. 1954. Closed 1964.*

map ref. 2   *The same building 1994.*

map ref. 3   *The Harrow 1953.*   *(courtesy: Colin Glover)*

map ref. 3   *Maggie's 1994.*

The Burtons Arms, c. 1966   Demolished 1973.
map ref. 4   *(courtesy: Whitbread Archive)*

The Yorkshire Grey, c. 1950. Demolished 1959.   *(courtesy: Greene King)*
map ref. 5

map ref. 6   *The Freeholder, c. 1955.*

map ref. 6   *The Freeholder 1994.*

map ref. 7   *The Painters Arms, c. 1930.*   *(courtesy: Benskins)*

map ref. 7   *The Painters Arms 1994.*

The Green Man, c. 1942.   *(courtesy: Connie Hannell)*
map ref. 8

map ref. 8   *The Green Man 1994.*

map ref. 8   *The lounge bar of the Green Man, c. 1942.*   *(courtesy: Connie Hannell)*

The public bar of the Green Man, c. 1950. Luton Town footballers in a darts match against the pub team. From left to right: Tommy Kieman, Jim Pemberton, unknown (partly hidden), Bob Wyldes, Lawrence Lawton, Jack Taylor, Willie Davie, George Stobbart (about to remove the darts), and standing far right is the publican Jesse Hannell.   *(courtesy: Connie Hannell)*

map ref. 8

The Welcome Stranger, c. 1953. Demolished 1958.
map ref. 9   *(courtesy: Colin Glover)*

The Britannia, c. 1953. Demolished 1958.
map ref. 10   *(courtesy: Colin Glover)*

map ref. 11　　　*The Bricklayers Arms, c. 1953.*　　　*(courtesy: Colin Glover)*

map ref. 11　　　　　*The Bricklayers Arms 1994.*

map ref. 12   *The Railway Inn, c. 1940.*

map ref. 12   *The Railway Tavern 1994.*

map ref. 13   *The Blockers Arms, c. 1953.*   *(courtesy: Colin Glover)*

map ref. 13   *The Blockers Arms 1994.*

map ref. 15   *The Rabbit, c. 1935.*

map ref. 15   *The Wabbit 1994.*

map ref. 15   *The sign on the current house.*

The North Star, c. 1960. Demolished about 1969.   *(courtesy: Whitbread Archive)*
map ref. 14

The Royal Hotel, c. 1930. Before reconstruction.   *(courtesy: Benskins)*
map ref. 16

map ref. 16   *The Royal under its present guise 'Taboo'.*

The Gardeners Call, c. 1955
map ref. 17

(courtesy: Greene King)

map ref. 17   *The Gardeners Call 1994.*

ROUND GREEN
and
STOPSLEY

There have been settlements at Round Green and Stopsley since at least the medieval period and it has even been recorded that there was a farmstead at Butterfield Green as early as the fourth century AD. These settlements were to grow slowly into villages and it is only comparatively recently that they have been included into the Borough of Luton.

Although Round Green is treated separately as a village, it formed part of the parish of Stopsley until 1928. The parish reached from Warden Hill, in the region of South Beds. Golf Clubhouse, in the north, to Someries in the south. The other borders were the county boundary at Putteridge, and a line roughly along the Old Bedford Road, then to Hart Lane and across what is now Luton Airport.

The older inhabitants of these former hamlets still tend to cling to the idea that their locality remains separate from the town of Luton and are very proud of the fact. Both hamlets have much to commend themselves and in their make-up are very typical of the village layout. Both had village greens, Stopsley boasting two, surrounded by the earliest dwellings, the church and, of course, the public houses.

Round Green has had three public houses trading on their original sites since at least the 1850s, but it is possible that two earlier inns were trading on the sites of *The Jolly Topers* and *The Shepherd and Flock*.

The village was very slow to develop, from the time when its main forms of employment were agriculture, in-house strawplaiting and the excavation of clay for the purpose of brick making. At the turn of the century there were fewer than a hundred properties in the village and, apart from travellers using the Luton to Hitchin road, it is almost certain that the public houses served only the local inhabitants.

Round Green, more so than Stopsley, has now become an extension of Luton, a trend that began when the tram service opened in 1907 with the eastern terminus of the system sited by the green outside *The Jolly Topers* public house. This enabled the inhabitants to travel easily into Luton in the search for work and it also opened up the delights of a rural setting for the Lutonians, not to mention the delights of the pubs. According to historian John Dony, some of Luton's 'wags' went so far as to nickname Round Green 'Wet End'. Even then it was a familiar sight to see sheep grazing alongside the electric giants of the modern world, two greatly contrasting views for the people not long out of the Victorian age.

241

Less than a mile to the east stands Stopsley, with its two greens. The main green lay in front of Pond Farm, where bonfires would be built on Guy Fawkes night and games of cricket were played. The smaller green, known to the older inhabitants as Chapel Green or Well Green after a communal well that had been there, was opposite *The Sportsman* public house. It was too small for socialising and the playing of games, so it seemed right and proper to erect the war memorial there after the Great War. The well is still there, with the war memorial built directly over the bore. There is no trace of grass left from this green in today's Stopsley.

Surrounded by the church and three pubs, Well Green stood at the centre of the old village. Some development took place around the larger green, particularly along Putteridge Road, to augment some existing buildings that stood at that end of the village.

During the first half of the nineteenth century, Stopsley boasted three public houses and one beerhouse. A public house named *The White Horse* stood by the main green on the Hitchin Road. It had stables to the rear and an arch to enable coaches to pull in. It was closed and pulled down around 1880 and some cottages were built on the site. These cottages are still standing, and the one which directly replaced *The White Horse* has recently been altered to provide an arch as access to a rear car park. Whether this was done with the old pub design in mind is doubtful but it does imitate the old house.

Stopsley remained much the same until after the end of the last war when the village began to expand, with the addition of new estates alongside the Hitchin Road and Wigmore Road. This development, with its additional population increase, necessitated the building of two new public houses, *The Double Barrel* and *The Hansom Cab*.

With the 1980s, and the building of a huge new estate to the south and east of Wigmore Road or Lane, another public house has been opened as part of the shopping centre close to the airport boundary.

1   The Royal Oak, 370 Hitchin Road

Trading in 1845 as an unnamed beerhouse for Messrs. Burr, and occupied by Edward Parrott. By 1870 it was owned by Thomas Sworder and was at that time occupied by George Cumberland. It now comes under the ownership of Courage.

2   The Shepherd and Flock, 386 Hitchin Road

This inn has been trading since at least 1840. It was purchased in 1862 by Simpson's Brewery of Baldock and by 1876 the tenant was Samuel Hyde.

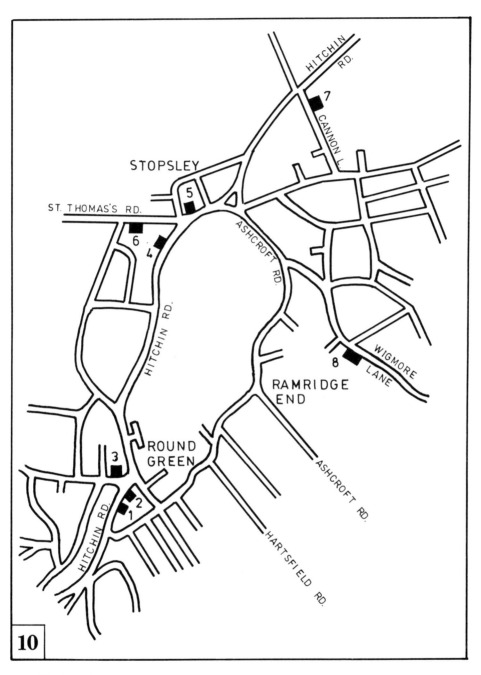

1 The Royal Oak
2 The Shepherd and Flock
3 The Jolly Topers
4 The First and Last
5 The Sportsman
6 The Brickmakers Arms
7 The Barrels
8 The Hansom Cab

The house remained under Simpson's ownership until the company was purchased by Greene King in 1954. It still remains trading for the company.

3 The Jolly Topers, Hitchin Road

There is mention of a house by this name in 1822 and by 1840 it was owned by John Steed of Baldock. Thirty years later the owner is listed as George Lines of Shillington, but sometime before 1898 it was acquired by William Pickering and supplied from Baldock by the Pale Ale Brewery.

In 1904 the brewery was calling itself the Baldock Brewery Company, and it was under this banner when Wells and Winch stepped in and purchased the lease. They finally bought the property from George Sibley in 1946.

Wells and Winch Brewery amalgamated with Greene King in 1961 and the public house remains with the company to this day.

The property was extensively modernised and renovated during 1989 when Greene King spent over £200,000 on refurbishment, which included incorporating the former off-licence next door into the main drinking area.

4 The First and Last, 587 Hitchin Road

Rebuilt around 1930, on the site of the original public house. Standing next to the Anglican church, the pub was aptly named, for at the time of its building it was the first dwelling house one would pass when entering the village or the last when leaving.

During the first two decades of this century it was populated by the more boisterous element of the village, while the wives of the customers were not allowed to be served in the bars and had to be content with the back kitchen.

The house became a very popular meeting place for the younger set during the 1960s. It is currently owned by Frederick King.

5 The Sportsman, Hitchin Road

The oldest surviving building of Stopsley's four licenced premises, being basically as built, with the addition of new windows at the front. Probably the most popular of the original three public houses, standing, where it does, facing the old Well Green.

By the 1870s it was owned by James Mardell of Harpenden, with

William Ransom in occupation. It came under the ownership of Glover and Sons, of Harpenden, in 1898, when they purchased Mardell's Peacock Brewery. It remained in Glover's hands until 1919, when they went into liquidation and the business was bought by J. W. Green.

It is said that King George the Fifth and Edward, Prince of Wales both had a drink in the saloon bar when they were attending a 'shoot' at nearby Putteridge Bury. The glasses they used were labelled as such and stood for many years on a special shelf behind the bar. Whatever became of them in the end is not known, but they are no longer in the pub. The validity of this story is open to conjecture, but it makes good telling.

6 The Brickmakers Arms, 45 St. Thomas's Road

This pub is most likely the unnamed beerhouse mentioned in the 1841 census returns. It was generally known as the 'Stopsley pub' and was given its present name when the Stopsley brick-fields began to take an ever increasing role in the village life.

During the 1870s it was owned by Edward Fordham of Ashwell, with the tenant being James Hawkins. It remained in Fordham's hands until the business was acquired by J. W. Green in 1952.

When *The Britannia* in Burr Street closed in 1957, the licensees Mr and Mrs Harris took over this house.

7 The Barrels, Cannon Lane

When the housing development between Putteridge Road and Hitchin Road began in the mid 1950s, it was realised that a public house was required at the eastern end of the village to serve the new community. Therefore, in 1962 the pub was built as a joint venture between Whitbread and A.B.C. and named *The Double Barrel*. The first two tenants were Robert Allen until 1966, followed by Eric Clements.

Late in 1989 Halls of Oxford took over for several months, reverting back to The Aylesbury Brewery Company for a month or two before coming under the banner of Ind Coope in March 1990, and renamed *The Barrels*.

8 The Hansom Cab, Wigmore Lane

The land on which the pub stands was purchased by Simpson's Brewery Ltd. in March 1938, but it was to be over twenty years before a public house was built on it. By March 1959, when it was opened, all Simpson's pubs and property, including land, had been acquired by Greene King, and so it was the first public house in Luton to be built and carry the Greene King logo from new. The licence was transferred from *The Yorkshire Grey* in High Town.

It has always been an extremely popular and busy house, partly due to the huge housing development that grew up around it, and to the fine ales that are kept there. The author celebrated his 'boys night out' in this pub before his marriage in 1975.

map ref. 1   *The Royal Oak, c. 1953.*   *(courtesy: Colin Glover)*

map ref. 1   *The Royal Oak 1994.*

map ref. 2   *The Shepherd and Flock, c. 1930.*   *(courtesy: Greene King)*

map ref. 2   *The Shepherd and Flock 1994.*

The village green and The Jolly Topers, c. 1910.   *(courtesy: Ken Cooper)*
map ref. 3

map ref. 3   *The Jolly Topers 1994.*

map ref. 4 *The First and Last 1965.* *(courtesy: Whitbread Archive)*

map ref. 4 *The First and Last 1994.*

map ref. 5   *The Sportsman, c. 1930.*   *(courtesy: James Dyer)*

map ref. 5   *Similar view to above, 1994.*

251

The Brickmakers Arms 1963.   *(courtesy: Whitbread Archive)*
map ref. 6

View across the main green. The building incorporating the arch was built around
1880 on the site of The White Horse public house.
map ref. 6

map ref. 7   *The Barrels 1994.*

The Hansom Cab, c. 1960.   *(courtesy: Greene King)*
map ref. 8

DALLOW, DUNSTABLE
and
LEAGRAVE ROADS

Although the three main roads covered in this section date from antiquity, only one of the eight public houses has any long history behind it. Apart from *The Fox*, the other seven have all arrived on the scene during the last sixty years.

1   The Fox, 32 to 34 Dunstable Road

First found mention two hundred years ago in 1794, standing in Dunstable Lane. Originally the inn was formed by three thatched cottages standing well back from the lane and facing the track to Dallow Farm.

The area in front of the inn was the site of an annual fair called 'Fox Fair', noted for its buns, called 'Wigs'. The inn sign featured the words:

> *'I am a Fox you plainly see*
> *There can no harm be found in me*
> *For Lawrence Clarke hath set me here*
> *To let you know he sells good beer'*

Lawrence Clarke was the innkeeper of this, one of the last inhabited houses in Luton, apart from farms and agricultural workers' cottages, before a traveller reached Dunstable. In 1842, the inn and the land each side of it was owned by Messrs. Burr with the inn occupied by Thomas Brown.

In 1925 the old inn was pulled down and a new building erected, this time adjacent to the main road. The resulting house was in a very attractive Tudor style, with exposed beams and stone window openings. The building was built in red brick, which was continued to the rear garden where the bricks were used in many walls and steps to make an attractive setting.

The pub was demolished in 1976 to make way for the Dunstable Road–Telford Way redevelopment and the overhead pedestrian walkway. During demolition some of the building materials were saved and re-used to build a new private house that was in the process of erection. The two carved fox heads, in particular, were carefully re-sited each side of the front bay window and possibly look more in place than in their original position.

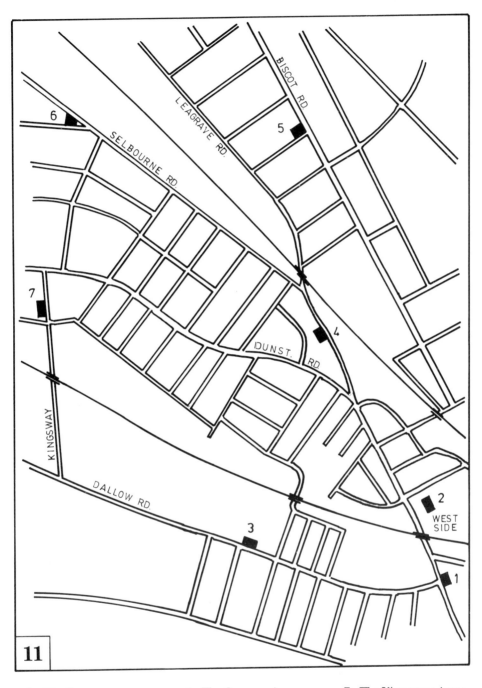

11

1 *The Fox*	4 *The Conway Arms*	7 *The Kingsway Arms*
2 *Nelson's Flagship*	5 *The Britannia*	8 *The Leicester Arms*
3 *The Bedfordshire Yeoman*	6 *The Salisbury Arms*	

2 Nelson's Flagship, West Side Centre

Opened on May 17th 1972 by Whitbread, and built on the site of Luton's old Gas Works. It was included as part of the new West Side shopping area which was intended to bring supermarkets and a variety of shops to the neglected west end side of the town.

The original name of the pub was *The Dutchman* and the interior fittings and decor were of a Dutch theme, with many of the furnishing and fittings made in Holland. The female bar staff were dressed in authentic Volendam costumes, while the men wore typical barmen's aprons.

The exterior was faced with small bricks to give a Flemish appearance and that appearance was enhanced by authentic red and white diamond-patterned shutters and striped Continental canopies over the windows. The forecourt signpost featured a life size Dutchman, complete with pipe and clogs.

The first managers were Mr and Mrs E. Ackland who had moved from the nearby *Fox*.

Unfortunately, the West Side Centre suffered from poor trade and the site, except for the pub, was demolished in the late 1980s, and replaced by a casino and a new supermarket. The pub was renamed *Nelson's Flagship* at about this time.

3 The Bedfordshire Yeoman, 214 Dallow Road

Opened on 13th December 1967 as a joint venture between Greene King and Whitbread. It is now under the control of Greene King.

4 The Conway Arms, 69 Leagrave Road

A Charles Wells public house since opening in May 1974 with the first tenant being Herbert Crowsley. It featured three bars, a public bar with games annexe, a saloon and a lounge bar.

It has always enjoyed a vigorous, busy trade.

5 The Britannia, Biscot Road

Opened by Flowers Breweries in July 1960, the licence was transferred from the recently closed *Horse and Jockey* in Manchester Street. The licensees, Mr and Mrs Sneddon, also moved to the new house.

6 The Salisbury Arms, 215 Selbourne Road

Built and opened as a Flowers house in December 1957. The name of the house had formerly graced the pub in Wellington Street destroyed by bombing in the last war. Between 1979 and 1982 Derrick and Cathy Fletcher were in occupation.

Standing close to the Selbourne Road industrial estate, the pub has always boasted a good lunchtime trade from the office and factory workers. The lunch menu is very varied and value for money.

7 The Kingsway Arms, Kingsway

Built by J. W. Green in the mid 1930s and opened in March 1936 as *The Kingsway Tavern*, a large typical pre-war style public house.

It was extensively modernised in the early 1980s and renamed *Champions*, to commemorate the promotion of Luton Town football club to the first division of the Football League (April 1982). At that time it featured an open plan split-level design, reminiscent of a night club and was owned by Whitbread Inns.

It has recently been renamed *The Kingsway Arms*.

8 The Leicester Arms, 581 Dunstable Road

As housing development continued to reach further away from the town centre towards Dunstable, in the early 1930s, it was realised that there was a need for a public house to keep pace with the ever increasing population. In 1933 *The Leicester Arms* was built, on similar lines to *The Kingsway*. It was to remain basically unaltered for around thirty-nine years, until 1972 when it was given an expensive internal renovation by the brewers Truman, and renamed *The Truman Gateway*. This change seemed to work, for throughout the 1970s it became the 'In' place to be for the younger set.

It has now settled down with a regular customer base and is currently owned and supplied by Bass Charrington.

The Fox public house, c. 1962. It was demolished in 1976. Notice the fox head carvings beneath the Flowers sign.
map ref. 1

The Fox lives! When the public house was demolished much of the building material was used to build this Luton house. The two fox carvings, in particular, have been tastefully included as shown.
map ref. 1

map ref. 2   *Nelson's Flagship 1994.*

map ref. 3   *The Bedfordshire Yeoman 1994.*

map ref. 4   *The Conway Arms 1994.*

map ref. 5   *The Britannia, c. 1960.*   *(courtesy: Whitbread Archive)*

map ref. 5   *The Britannia 1994.*

map ref. 6   *The Salisbury Arms, c. 1958.*   *(courtesy: Whitbread Archive)*

map ref. 6   *The Salisbury Arms 1994.*

map ref. 7   *The Kingsway Tavern, c. 1953.*   *(courtesy: Colin Glover)*

map ref. 7   *The Kingsway Arms 1994.*

map ref. 8   *The Leicester Arms 1994.*

The lounge bar of the Salisbury Arms, c. 1980.   *(courtesy: Derrick Fletcher)*
map ref. 6

BISCOT
and
LIMBURY

These two old hamlets have a similar history to that of Round Green and Stopsley, having been mainly involved with agriculture for most of their past. Both have now been extensively developed to provide housing for the ever growing town, and where they were both entirely separate from Luton, they are now well and truly part of this large cosmopolitan area.

The old original centre of Biscot lay in the vicinity of Trinity Road and Moat Lane, with Limbury centred on Black Swan Lane, Neville Road and Kingsley Road.

There is no recorded fact of Biscot ever boasting a public house, while neighbouring Limbury had two licenced premises, within a stone's throw of each other. Many of the public houses covered in this section cannot strictly be considered as being in Biscot and Limbury, having been built on the new estates to the north of the hamlets, but are included as they serve both of the communities.

1   Biscot Mill, Biscot Road

Built in 1958, on the site of Luton's longest surviving windmill. The brewers Mann, Crossman and Paulin surrendered the licences of *The Albion* in Ebenezer Street and *The Welcome Stranger* in Duke Street in order to gain a new licence and permission to build this house.

As a reminder that the house stands on the site of the windmill, there are a couple of old millstones set into the flagstones at the front of the inn.

It occupies a prominent position and was an extremely large house for its time, with large bars and featuring a function room to the side and rear. This room was very popular for wedding receptions as well as a regular venue, during the 1960s, for the Musicians Union monthly dances.

During the 1980s the house was converted into a carvery bar, trading under the name *Barnaby's Carvery*, but within the last couple of years the restaurant side of the business has closed and the eating area to the rear is currently standing empty and unused.

2   The Wheatsheaf, 184 Bishopscote Road

Built and opened by Flowers in July 1960, and took over the name of the public house demolished in Church Street a few years before.

A Whitbread house that features live music twice each week.

3   The Moat House, Moat Lane

Built around 1370 as the manor house for the Bereford family, and as such is the oldest secular building in south Bedfordshire, ante-dating the brick gatehouse and chapel at Someries by over a century.

The building stands inside a moat which is possibly of a later date, some of this moat having been brick lined during the early eighteenth century. The walls of the house, which are made from Totternhoe stone, chalkblock and flint rubble, are three feet thick and exist to a height of sixteen feet. Early in the seventeenth century the house was open to the roof with a central hearth, but it was then divided horizontally with a first floor and ceilings, and provided with stairs. A huge chimney stack, typical of its period, was then required.

During the 1950s the house began to fall into disrepair and there was some danger of it being demolished but, due to its history, it was a relief when the Creasey family took over, and after tasteful renovation they opened the building as a public house and restaurant during 1969. A large banquet hall, built in the same style, was opened to the rear to provide a function room and carvery.

Now a Charringtons house and one of the busiest pubs in the town.

4   The Black Swan, Black Swan Lane

In 1824 this inn was already trading under the name of *The Swan*. In 1845 it was under the tenancy of Richard Stokes, and by 1876, it was under the ownership of the Lucas Brothers of Hitchin, and was to stay with them until their brewery was bought out, in 1921, by J. W. Green.

When owned by Lucas Brothers, the inn was destroyed by fire, around 1900, it was rebuilt and renamed *The Black Swan*. It remained as built until the family room was added during the mid 1980s. The house has always been popular and boasts of a hard core regular clientele, now with the addition of families using the recent facilities.

1 The Biscot Mill
2 The Wheatsheaf
3 The Moat House
4 The Black Swan

5 The Bird in Hand
6 The Heron
7 The Boater
8 The Warden

9 The Roman Legion
10 The Purley Tavern
11 The Bird and Bush
     (not on map)

5   The Bird in Hand, Black Swan Lane

A little known beerhouse that stood in the triangle formed by Black
Swan Lane, then called Water Lane, Neville Passage and Neville Road,
then called Milton Road. It was run by James Fensome in 1845, but its
antiquity is unknown. It saw its last days just before the turn of the
century, when it was pulled down.

6   The Heron, Watermead Road

Built by Whitbread and opened on 4th April 1962 to serve the
developing Limbury Mead estate. The licence was transferred from *The
Royal Oak* in Windsor Street which closed in March of that year.

This is another public house to recognise the need for family
accommodation with the addition of a family room and large safe
garden. The garden is used every November 5th for a giant free bonfire
and fireworks party which attracts hundreds of visitors.

7   The Boater, Icknield Way

Built in 1962 by Greene King and opened just before Christmas that
year. The licence was transferred from *The Midland Hotel*, first to *The
Centurion* in Dunstable in 1961, and then to *The Boater* in time for the
opening. The first tenant was Edward Horn, followed by his wife Joan
until 1979. For the next seven years, Francis Brannigan and Walter
Sidney Ford ran the house in turn.

The extensive range of fine ales and friendly atmosphere has always
attracted a good custom. In 1987 it underwent a major overhaul, not
only to the structure but a complete refit of the interior as well. At the
time of the renovation the landlord was Patrick Maguire, the well
known local boxer.

It has since had more internal refits and now features regular quiz
nights, which are very well attended.

8   The Warden, 129 Barton Road

Opened in February 1939 as *The Wardown Tavern*, later to be changed to
The Warden Tavern. It underwent much renovation and enlargement
during the early 1980s with the addition of a large restaurant area. Its
name was changed to the current one around 1985 and it is still owned
by Whitbread and run as a Beefeater Restaurant.

9 The Roman Legion, Whitehorse Vale

Opened by Charles Wells in July 1986 to cope with the expanding Barton Hills development. The first occupiers of this pleasant and typical new estate public house were Derek Charles Gibbs and Brian William Hunt. The pub is just beginning to stabilise its regular customer base.

10 The Purley Tavern, The Purley Centre

Built as part of the Purley Centre shopping complex in 1974 in what was then the new Marsh Farm development.

It was at first called *The Cotters*, after a medieval agricultural worker, when its owners Watney Mann organised a competition to find an original name for their new house. A Mr and Mrs Fensome of Luton won the competition with the prize of free beer for a year.

During the late 1970s and early 1980s live music was a regular attraction at the pub and it would be packed with customers on those nights. Later, unfortunately, an undesirable element started to frequent the house and trade suffered badly.

After a face-lift and name change to *The Moakes* business picked up and it now enjoys a steady trade. It had another name change around 1992 to its present title.

11 Bird and Bush, Hancock Drive, Bushmead

Before the opening of *Yates's Wine Lodge* this was Luton's newest public house having opened during 1993. Built to serve the new Bushmead estate and forms part of the Bushmead shopping precinct. An attractive property from the outside and a very friendly atmosphere inside.

map ref. 1   *The Biscot Mill 1994.*

map ref. 2   *The Wheatsheaf 1994.*

map ref. 3   *The old moat farm when standing empty, c. 1957.*

map ref. 3   *The Moat House 1994.*

map ref. 4   *The Black Swan, c. 1950.*

map ref. 4   *The Black Swan 1994.*

map ref. 6   *The Heron 1994.*

map ref. 7   *The Boater 1994.*

map ref. 8 *The Warden 1994.*

map ref. 9 *The Roman Legion 1994.*

map ref. 10   *The Purley Tavern 1994.*

map ref. 11   *The Bird and Bush 1994.*

LEAGRAVE

Travellers and settlers knew the area that was to become Leagrave from at least the Mesolithic or Middle Stone Age. Mesolithic man inhabited the Leagrave area, possibly living in hollows scooped in the river gravels, sheltered with branches and skins. A pick-like Mesolithic tool was found during excavations beside Leagrave Marsh over forty years ago. The ancient trackway known as the Icknield Way ran across the area, and some 3,000 years BC the first people decided to settle beside the springs of the river Lea. The Romans settled close by and remains of their houses have been discovered in the Runfold and Bramingham Road areas.

The settlement slowly grew, but the name of Leagrave is relatively modern, as the name was virtually unknown two hundred years ago. In a case that came before the 1227 Assize 'Nicholas de Littlegrave and Herbert de Littlegrave' found mention, and the many varying forms of the name have suggested that Leagrave was originally called 'Lihtlan graf' (Lihtla's grave).

Public houses or beerhouses have been thought to exist since at least 1765. The Leagrave of one hundred and fifty years ago possessed three licenced premises, a figure which was to remain as such until the early 1960s, when large housing developments at Lewsey and Sundon Park necessitated the building of three more pubs.

In 1844 the village stretched from Compton Avenue to Partridge Farm (on the site of the M1 bridge), most properties being farms and farm workers' cottages. There were also a few buildings clustered around *The Three Horse Shoes* public house and sheep dip close to the river crossing.

1   The Three Horse Shoes, Marsh Road

Included in Leagrave for the old licencing list although strictly speaking in Limbury. The house gained its first mention in 1811 and in the 1822 licencing list it was in the name of Thomas Wilson who was bound over for £30 to fulfil his licence. Twenty years later George Read was in occupation.

It is possible that the building was some years older as, when in 1938 the old building was being demolished by Messrs. A. W. Oakley Ltd. workmen found graffiti on the walls with the date 1796. As this date was seen in four different places, there are strong reasons to suspect that the building was used as an ale house from at least this date. Situated next to the sheep dip and on the old Icknield Way, it would have been a very

1 The Three Horse Shoes
2 The Sugar Loaf
3 The Royal Oak
4 The Man On Wheels
5 The Favourite
6 The Roman Way
   (not on map)
7 The Unicorn (not on map)

to the sheep dip and on the old Icknield Way, it would have been a very popular inn with the shepherds, drovers and travellers.

By 1876 it was owned by Elizabeth Healey of Harpenden, although she had leased her brewery to Benjamin Bennett. The inn came under the ownership of Mardalls in 1893 and then Glover and Sons of Harpenden in 1898. When this company went into liquidation during 1919, J. W. Green purchased the brewery and all its pubs.

After the old house was demolished in 1938, Green's rebuilt on the same site but on a much grander scale. The new pub featured large spacious bars and function facilities attached to the lounge area. For the last few years of its active life it served as a social club for Whitbread employees. It was closed around 1984 and after standing empty and suffering from vandalism the building was finally demolished in 1995. There had been a concerted effort to keep the building and re-open as a public house but all these efforts came to nothing. Neville's, the builders and undertakers, took it upon themselves to try and preserve some of the history of the pub by erecting the pub sign in the middle of the roundabout adjacent to their offices. This was done at their own expense and they can only be praised for their efforts.

2 The Sugar Loaf, High Street

Has been trading since at least 1845, when it was owned by the Lucas Brothers of Hitchin, and the tenant was Thomas Stokes, the brother of Richard Stokes, who was at that time tenant of *The Black Swan* at Limbury.

From 1880 a horse-bus service was operated between *The Sugar Loaf* and Luton, transporting workers mainly involved in the hat trade. At the beginning of this century, the service was run by 'Topper Cain', and by 1909, a daily motor bus service was instituted, by Balfour Beatty Ltd., to ply from *The Sugar Loaf* to Bury Park, it being the first regular motorbus service. This faster service meant the death of Cain's horse-bus which was left to slowly fall to pieces in Strange's farmyard.

In 1921, J. W. Green took over the Lucas brewery and the pub remained in his hands before changing to Flowers and later to Whitbread ownership.

3 The Royal Oak, Oakley road

Although the first official reference to this beerhouse appears in 1822, under the name of Samuel Wright, it appears to have existed either as a private house or beerhouse as it is shown on Jeffrey's map dated 1765.

It was a small thatched building standing on the edge of Backside field in a tree lined lane that was to become known as Oak Road. It was small pantry and kitchen, a cellar with cask entrance and two small bedrooms.

In 1830 its opening hours were established by Act 'not to be open before Four in the morning nor after Ten in the evening, nor on Sundays between Ten and One or Three and Five in the day'. It was intended that this Act would cater for the agricultural workers, for whom beer was a vital part of their diet and an integral part of their wages.

Even with these opening hours, David Low of *The Royal Oak* was charged with selling beer between the hours of Three and Five on the afternoon of Sunday 12th October 1856.

In 1851 the publican's son, William Low, plied a twice weekly coach run to London, leaving *The Royal Oak* at 3 p.m., on Mondays and Thursdays, arriving at Aldergate Street, London at 5 o'clock the next morning. He would begin the return journey at 3 p.m., arriving in Luton at 11 a.m. the next morning.

By 1861 William was described as 'London carrier, employer of two men'. Early owners of this inn had been Messrs. Burr, followed by Benskins of Watford. By 1876 Thomas Sworder was owner with William Low in occupation. When Sworder's brewery was acquired by J. W. Green in 1897, he soon demolished the old house and built the one that still stands today.

4   The Man On Wheels, Acworth Crescent

Built and opened in 1969 to serve the large Hockwell Ring development which had been without a local public house since the estate was first laid out during the early 1960s. The interior decor was tastefully carried out with a wooden ceiling and exposed brickwork. There was an outside sitting and barbecue area with ample car parking. The first tenant was Mr George Albert Reed and for the first ten years or so after opening the pub plied its trade with no more than the normal problems associated with a busy estate public house. From 1982 Derrick and Cathy Fletcher took over as tenants after having previously been in charge at *The Freeholder*, *The Blacksmiths Arms* and *The Salisbury*. The reliable regulars in the pub were instrumental in organising many charity events, including helping local pensioners to take a holiday in Spain. Unfortunately, there were also problems with an undesirable element among some of its customers with the police being called in on numerous occasions to deal with rowdy and violent incidents. It was also believed that a certain amount of drug dealing was taking place, resulting in the police keeping a close watch on the premises, sometimes concealed in the front bedrooms of private houses overlooking the pub. In November 1986 a brawl broke out involving over fifty people resulting in some being taken to hospital, Mr Fletcher being one of the cases. The patience of the police, Whitbread's and the local inhabitants had been stretched to the limit, resulting in the pub closing its doors in December 1986. Mr and Mrs Fletcher left on December 7th to take over at *The Engine*, where they were to remain until their retirement in 1994.

The Man On Wheels remained closed over the Christmas and New Year period and reopened in January with temporary managers. It proved to be unsuccessful and, following more incidents, Whitbread surrendered the licence on March 20th 1987. The building stood empty for about two years, gradually falling into total disrepair, before the site was sold for redevelopment and the building was demolished in 1990, the first pub to be knocked down since *The Fox* in 1976.

5   The Favourite, Sundon Park Road

Built by Whitbread in 1962, at a time when so many others were opening, to deal with the post war population explosion. The first tenants were Robert Allen and Dennis Jefferies. This house was built for the Sundon Park development and has been a very popular pub since. The pub has for many years featured live music in the form of rock and pop bands and has prided itself on the quality of its football, darts and pool teams.

6   The Roman Way, Tomlinson Avenue

Opened in October 1965, by Bass Charrington, when the eastern end of the Leagrave High Street development was completed. To this day it remains the property of Charrington's.

7   The Unicorn, Wheatfield Road

Opened within a year of *The Roman Way* in May 1966 and is the most eastern public house in Luton, standing only a few hundred metres from the boundary with Dunstable. It featured in the news during 1970 when Luton Town footballer Graham French had an altercation with another local man, which ended with French shooting the other man outside the premises. French subsequently served a prison sentence.

The junction of Marsh Road and Bramingham Road. Taken at the beginning of this century and clearly showing the prominent position occupied by the old Three Horse Shoes public house.

map ref. 1

The original Three Horse Shoes, c. 1910. It was demolished during 1938.
map ref. 1

The Three Horse Shoes, c. 1910. From 1898 to 1919 it was under the ownership of Glover and sons.

map ref. 1

The Three Horse Shoes and the river Lea, c. 1914. This view from Marsh Farm House shows the area of the sheep dip and 'sands' known as the Blockers' Seaside.
map ref. 1

The Three Horse Shoes, c. 1954. It was built in 1938 on the site of the original house. It is currently in the process of demolition (Feb. 1995).
map ref. 1

283

map ref. 2   *The Sugar Loaf, c. 1950.*

map ref. 2   *The Sugar Loaf 1994.*

The original Royal Oak, c. 1899. Demolished and rebuilt 1900.

map ref. 3

map ref. 3   *The rebuilt Royal Oak 1994.*

map ref. 5   *The Favourite 1994.*

Official opening day of The Man On Wheels, 1969.   *(courtesy: John Lee)*
map ref. 4

The Man on Wheels' lounge bar 1982.   *(courtesy: Derrick Fletcher)*
map ref. 4

Derrick Fletcher of The Man On Wheels 1982 to 1986.   *(courtesy: Derrick Fletcher)*
map ref. 4

map ref. 6   *The Roman Way 1994.*

map ref. 7   *The Unicorn 1994.*

SOUTH EAST LUTON

This south east corner of Luton had been agricultural land and occupied by farmsteads until the 1930s, consequently none of the public houses featured in this section are much older than half a century. Most of the land in this area had been owned by the wealthy Crawley family since the seventeenth century. They had also owned Someries since 1629.

At the turn of this century, the only roads in existence, shown on the map, were Crawley Green Road, Eaton Green Road, Somerset Avenue and Ashcroft Road, the last two being only unmade tracks. The nearest habitations of any note were those at Round Green and in Lea Road.

There were four substantial farms, Wigmore Hall, Eaton Green Farm, now the site of Luton Airport, Crawley Green Farm and Nether Crawley.

Wigmore Hall is now a licenced hotel and function room. Eaton Green farmhouse was used as the headquarters of Luton Flying Club, until the present club was opened, and consequently had a drinks licence. The farmhouse of Crawley Green Farm is now the clubhouse of the Royal Naval Club, licenced of course. Nether Crawley farm was situated on Crawley Green Road on the lower corner of what was to become Somerset Avenue. In its last years, before being pulled down in the 1960s, it was owned by a Mrs Hartop. The story has it that the farm was owned by the Cooper family, ancestors of Luton historian, Ken Cooper, and that the farm was lost to the Crawley family, as a wager, during a game of cards!

There was an ancient inn, known as *The Tin Pot*, situated in the old hamlet of Crawley Green. The location of this hamlet, now entirely built over, was between the clubhouse of the Royal Naval Club and the junction of Crawley Green Road and Devon Road. It consisted of the inn and a group of cottages positioned around the green. By 1963 all that remained of this ancient hamlet was a couple of cottages which were occupied by farm workers on the Powdrill Farm Estate. The inn was described by Austin as 'seventeenth century and the resort of the sporting fraternity'. Davis's 'History of Luton' records that the hamlet belonged to the Abbey of St. Albans and that the inn was the site for the 'sports' of bull and horse baiting. He also said that as late as 1874 traces of the baiting ring were still visible.

There was much building development in this area during the years leading up to the second war. Mr Powdrill, of Crawley Green Farm, commissioned two local builders, H. C. Janes and Jayes, to build a selection of terraced houses on his land, which included the whole of Crawley Green Road. At the same time, the development of Somerset Avenue, Walcot Avenue and parts of Holly Bush Road and Eaton Green Road was taking place. After the war, when building restrictions were lifted, the Abbots Wood Road estate and the steel houses of Hartsfield Road, Burnham Road, etc. were erected, for an expected life of no more than twenty years. They are still standing, a tribute to the high standard of design and of the materials used. The area was known then, and still is, as 'Tin Town'.

During the war, the airport estate, bounded by Holly Bush Road and Lalleford Road, was one vast open field. The elevation of this field was such that an anti-aircraft gun emplacement was sited there to complement another at Wigmore Hall. The latter is still in existence, with the gunners' accommodation now housing a bat colony.

The airport estate was developed during the late fifties and early sixties, and building is still taking place around Wigmore Lane.

1   The Somerset Tavern, 263 Crawley Green Road

Built and opened by J. W. Green around 1938. The building is very large and imposing, standing, as it does, above the road level. It consists of a large public bar, lounge and function room to the rear. There is a beer terrace all the way round the front aspect, overlooking the car park and road.

The first tenants were Mr and Mrs Bland, and they were to remain in the pub until the 1960s.

2   The Wyvern, Eaton Green Road

Opened in November 1953, when the licence was transferred from *The Dew Drop* in Upper George Street. It is a typical two bar public house of the post war period, and received much of its lunch time trade from the neighbouring Vauxhall and airport works.

3   The King Harry, Fermore Crescent

Opened on 23rd September 1964, when Sir Fordham Flower, Chairman of Flowers Breweries Ltd., performed the opening ceremony. The first pint was pulled by the Mayor of Luton, Cllr. Frank Beckett.

It replaced *The King Harry* in Hitchin Road which had closed the previous evening. The licence and licensee, Mr John Packman, both transferred to the new house.

It was designed by the Luton architects Messrs. Peter Dunham, Widdup and Harrison in association with Mr W. E. Edleston, Group Architect to Flowers Breweries Ltd.

It contains two spacious bars and ample sitting out terraces. The interior decor, when opened, had an 'Age of Kings' theme, and featured an attractive tapestry called 'Agincourt'.

The origin of the name King Harry was the name often given to Henry the Fifth, who succeeded his father, Henry the Fourth, in 1413. In two brilliant campaigns he brought France to her knees and defeated a French army three times larger than his own at the Battle of Agincourt, in 1415. Henry died in 1422 and was greatly mourned as a great king and fine soldier.

4   The Straw Plaiters, 323 Ashcroft Road

Opened in September 1968 to take advantage of the development to the east of Ashcroft Road which had been without a local since being built.

One of the three public houses to be named in connection with the straw hat industry, the others being *The Boater* and *The Panama*. It received its name as a result of a pub naming competition. Considering the history of Luton and the hat trade, it is surprising that there have not been more inn signs devoted to the theme.

5   The Wigmore Arms, Wigmore Lane

One of the town's newest public houses, having opened in 1991, to cope with the new estate that is still growing at the airport end of Stopsley.

It forms part of a shopping complex and is a typical 'estate establishment', quite spacious and modern with a good young atmosphere.

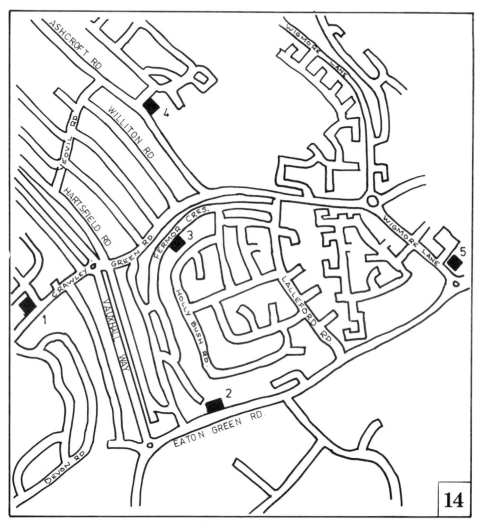

1 The Somerset Tavern   3 The King Harry   5 The Wigmore Arms
2 The Wyvern   4 The Straw Plaiters

map ref. 1   *The Somerset Tavern 1994.*

map ref. 2   *The Wyvern 1994.*

map ref. 3   *The King Harry 1994.*

map ref. 4   *The Straw Plaiters 1994.*

map ref. 5   *The Wigmore Arms 1994.*

OFF-LICENCES

The origins of the off-licence stem from the old style beerhouse, i.e. a house that was licensed to sell beer for consumption on the premises, but not spirits. In general, a beerhouse tended to be in the poorer areas, therefore catering for a more volatile and rougher element of the community, and subsequently tended to fall foul of the law, more so than the public house.

The Wine and Beerhouse Act of 1869, which at last restricted unlicensed premises, and the 1904 Licencing Act, which resulted in the non-renewal of many licences, particularly for troublesome premises, meant the closure of many beerhouses and public houses.

There is no doubt that some of those houses that had lost their licence later opened up as independent beershops and off-licences. The general trend though, was for the large breweries to operate their own wine and spirits retail business as well as to have off-sale retail outlets.

Flowers owned the off-licence chain of Threshers, which was acquired by Whitbread, in 1962, with the takeover. It is now Whitbread's main off-licence chain with 1,600 branches. The chain of Mackies is also under the Whitbread banner.

There are five trading styles under the Thresher banner – Thresher Wine Shops, Drink Stores from Thresher, Wine Rack, Food and Drinks Stores from Thresher and Bottoms Up, which became part of the Whitbread empire with the acquisition, in 1991, of Peter Dominic.

Westminster Wine Company was established by Watneys in 1929, as their first step in creating a chain of off-licences. It began with three shops in London, and now totals over two hundred nationwide. Watneys also have retail outlets through the Hammerton and Co. chain, as well as through individual Manns, Ushers, Phipps and Wilson's off-licences.

The Courage Group have off sales through the Arthur Cooper and Saccone and Speed off-licences.

There are very few of the old style off-licences, that have remained virtually unchanged over the years, in Luton. Two examples are the Sanderson shop, on the corner of Bury Park Road and Waldeck Road, which closed as recently as September 1994, and the Worlds End off-licence in New Town Street. The latter, having been a troublesome beerhouse in the 1860s, lost its licence after the 1869 beerhouse cull, reopening in 1870 as an off-licence.

There are many, of course, that are still trading on their original sites but have been dramatically altered. The modern trend is to feature large plate glass windows, enabling the owner or manager to have impressive product displays to catch the customers' attention.

Many of the old public houses had an off sales counter, with its own access of course, but these seem to have completely disappeared, with the space previously taken instead used to enhance the size of the in-house drinking area.

The following photographs feature a random selection of differing styles of off-licence. Some of the older ones have long been demolished, and several of the buildings are still standing, although trading under different businesses. Others feature the later style of premises which are familiar to all of us. I have made no attempt to feature any supermarket off-sales or indeed any of the many corner type grocers' shops that have a licence to sell intoxicating liquor.

Two off-licence premises in North Street. Both were demolished about 1970. Joseph Tabbron had been trading at number 26 since the late 1920s. Number 97, on the corner with William Street had been trading since at least 1930.

(both photographs courtesy: Whitbread Archive)

The Queen's Arms at 72 Wenlock Street, c. 1950. It was closed for business in the 1950s, and demolished in 1974. (courtesy: Whitbread Archive)

Number 27 Court Road, c. 1950. Demolished in 1960. On this junction with Vicarage Street stood a tobacconist, a Kosher food store and two off-licences. The other at number 29 was called The Granville, and was owned by the Bedford brewers Charles Wells. It was demolished in 1970, the business being transferred to the building adjacent to The White Lion. (courtesy: Whitbread Archive)

Number 30 Cardigan Street, c. 1930.
(courtesy: Whitbread Archive)

The same building 1994. The upper storey extension and ground level alterations have
been carried out since 1986. Before then, the building was much the same as in the
earlier photograph.

World's End off-licence, New Town Street, c. 1930. Previously a beerhouse under the same name.(courtesy: Whitbread Archive)

Still trading in the same business 1994

Sanderson's off-licence in Waldeck Road. Closed 1994.

This off-licence in Hart Lane has undergone very few changes and has been trading on this site for over forty years.

An example of a later style off-licence, although this one, in Calverton road, has been open for business for around twenty years.

305

Alphabetical Index

Books Published by THE BOOK CASTLE

JOURNEYS INTO HERTFORDSHIRE:
Anthony Mackay. Foreword by The Marquess of Salisbury, Hatfield House.
Nearly 200 superbly detailed ink drawings depict the towns, buildings and
landscape of this still predominantly rural county.

JOURNEYS INTO BEDFORDSHIRE:
Anthony Mackay. Foreword by The Marquess of Tavistock, Woburn Abbey.
A lavish book of over 150 evocative ink drawings.

**COUNTRYSIDE CYCLING IN BEDFORDSHIRE, BUCKINGHAMSHIRE
AND HERTFORDSHIRE:** Mick Payne.
Twenty rides on- and off-road for all the family.

LEAFING THROUGH LITERATURE:
Writers' Lives in Hertfordshire and Bedfordshire: David Carroll.
Illustrated short biographies of many famous authors and their connections
with these counties.

THROUGH VISITORS' EYES: A Bedfordshire Anthology:
edited by Simon Houfe.
Impressions of the county by famous visitors over the last four centuries,
thematically arranged and illustrated with line drawings.

THE HILL OF THE MARTYR: An Architectural History of St. Albans Abbey:
Eileen Roberts.
Scholarly and readable chronological narrative history of Hertfordshire and
Bedfordshire's famous cathedral. Fully illustrated with photographs and plans.

LOCAL WALKS : South Bedfordshire and North Chilterns: Vaughan Basham.
Twenty-seven thematic circular walks.

LOCAL WALKS : North and Mid-Bedfordshire: Vaughan Basham.
Twenty-five thematic circular walks.

**CHILTERN WALKS: Hertfordshire, Bedfordshire and
North Buckinghamshire:** Nick Moon.

CHILTERN WALKS: Buckinghamshire: Nick Moon.

CHILTERN WALKS: Oxfordshire and West Buckinghamshire: Nick Moon.
A trilogy of circular walks, in association with the Chiltern Society. Each
volume contains thirty circular walks.

OXFORDSHIRE WALKS: Oxford, the Cotswolds and the Cherwell Valley:
Nick Moon.

OXFORDSHIRE WALKS: Oxford, the Downs and the Thames Valley:
Nick Moon.
Two volumes that complement Chiltern Walks: Oxfordshire and complete
coverage of the county, in association with the Oxford Fieldpaths Society. Thirty
circular walks in each.

FOLK: Characters and Events in the History of Bedfordshire and Northamptonshire: Vivienne Evans.
Anthology about people of yesteryear – arranged alphabetically by village or town.

LEGACIES: Tales and Legends of Luton and the North Chilterns: Vic Lea.
Twenty-five mysteries and stories based on fact, including Luton Town Football Club. Many photographs.

ECHOES: Tales And Legends of Bedfordshire and Hertfordshire: Vic Lea.
Thirty, compulsively retold historical incidents.

MYTHS and WITCHES, PEOPLE and POLITICS:
Tales from Four Shires: Bucks., Beds., Herts., and Northants.: John Houghton.
Anthology of strange but true historical events.

ECCENTRICS and VILLAINS, HAUNTINGS and HEROES.:
Tales from Four Shires: Northants., Beds., Bucks. and Herts.: John Houghton.
True incidents and curious events covering one thousand years.

THE RAILWAY AGE IN BEDFORDSHIRE: Fred Cockman.
Classic, illustrated account of early railway history.

JOHN BUNYAN: HIS LIFE AND TIMES: Vivienne Evans.
Foreword by the Bishop of Bedford. Preface by Terry Waite.
Bedfordshire's most famous son set in his seventeenth century context.

SWANS IN MY KITCHEN: The Story of a Swan Sanctuary: Lis Dorer.
Foreword by Dr Philip Burton. Updated edition.
Tales of her dedication to the survival of these beautiful birds through her sanctuary near Hemel Hempstead.

WHIPSNADE WILD ANIMAL PARK: 'MY AFRICA': Lucy Pendar.
Foreword by Andrew Forbes. Introduction by Gerald Durrell.
Inside story of sixty years of the Park's animals and people – full of anecdotes, photographs and drawings.

DUNSTABLE WITH THE PRIORY, 1100–1550: Vivienne Evans.
Dramatic growth of Henry I's important new town around a major crossroads.

DUNSTABLE DECADE: THE EIGHTIES: – A Collection of Photographs:
Pat Lovering.
A souvenir book of nearly 300 pictures of people and events in the 1980s.

DUNSTABLE IN DETAIL: Nigel Benson.
A hundred of the town's buildings and features, plus town trail map.

OLD DUNSTABLE: Bill Twaddle.
A new edition of this collection of early photographs.

BOURNE AND BRED: A Dunstable Boyhood Between the Wars: Colin Bourne.
An elegantly written, well-illustrated book capturing the spirit of the town over fifty years ago.

ROYAL HOUGHTON: Pat Lovering.
Illustrated history of Houghton Regis from the earliest times to the present.

BEDFORDSHIRE'S YESTERYEARS Vol. 1: The Family,
Childhood and Schooldays: Brenda Fraser-Newstead.
Unusual early 20th century reminiscences, with private photographs.

BEDFORDSHIRE'S YESTERYEARS Vol 2: The Rural Scene:
Brenda Fraser-Newstead.
Vivid first-hand accounts of country life two or three generations ago.

THE CHANGING FACE OF LUTON: An Illustrated History:
Stephen Bunker, Robin Holgate and Marian Nichols.
Luton's development from earliest times to the present busy industrial town.
Illustrated in colour and monochrome. The three authors from Luton Museum
are all experts in local history, archaeology, crafts and social history.

THE MEN WHO WORE STRAW HELMETS: Policing Luton, 1840–1974:
Tom Madigan.
Meticulously chronicled history; dozens of rare photographs; author served
Luton Police for nearly fifty years.

BETWEEN THE HILLS: The Story of Lilley, a Chiltern Village: Roy Pinnock.
A priceless piece of our heritage – the rural beauty remains but the customs and
way of life described here have largely disappeared.

FARM OF MY CHILDHOOD, 1925–1947: Mary Roberts.
An almost vanished lifestyle on a remote farm near Flitwick.

THE TALL HITCHIN SERGEANT: A Victorian Crime Novel based on fact:
Edgar Newman.
Mixes real police officers and authentic background with an exciting storyline.

SPECIALLY FOR CHILDREN

VILLA BELOW THE KNOLLS: A Story of Roman Britain: Michael Dundrow.
An exciting adventure for young John in Totternhoe and Dunstable two
thousand years ago.

ADVENTURE ON THE KNOLLS: A Story of Iron Age Britain:
Michael Dundrow.
Excitement on Totternhoe Knolls as ten-year-old John finds himself back in
those dangerous times, confronting Julius Caesar and his army.

THE RAVENS: One Boy Against the Might of Rome: James Dyer.
On the Barton Hills and in the south-east of England as the men of the great fort
of Ravensburgh (near Hexton) confront the invaders.

Further titles are in preparation.
All the above are available via any bookshop, or from the publisher and bookseller
THE BOOK CASTLE
12 Church Street, Dunstable, Bedfordshire, LU5 4RU Tel: (01582) 605670

YOU'RE NOT FAR FROM THE FAYRE IN LUTON.

A Brewers Fayre. If you want great value food in relaxed, informal surroundings, you've just found it.

We're open all day, every day of the week. Offering everything from a quick snack, to a three course meal for

all the family. Find your nearest Brewers Fayre and you won't find better value or friendlier service anywhere.

WICKED LADY
Normansland Common, Wheathampstead. Near St. Albans.
Tel: 01582 832 128

KINGSTON TAVERN
40 Winchester Circle, Kingston Centre. Milton Keynes.
Tel: 01908 584371.

THREE HORSESHOES
616 Hatfield Road, Smallford, St. Albans Tel: 01727 851 608.

RED LION
High Street, Elstow, Near Bedford, Tel: 01234 359687.

ROYAL OAK
Chapelfoot, Langley, Near Hitchen. Tel: 01462 432 653

KINGS ARMS
The Green, Cardington, Bedford. Tel: 01234 838533.

OLD RED LION
Bidwell Hill, Houghton Regis, Dunstable. Tel: 01582 867439.

GIFFARD PARK
Broadway Avenue, Milton Keynes. Tel: 01908 210025.

COWPERS ARMS
Cole Green Lane, Cole Green, Near Hertford. Tel: 01707 330202.

WOLVERTON HOUSE
Statford Road, Wolverton Mill, Milton Keynes. Tel: 01908 26157

NOWHERE'S FAIRER
THAN A BREWERS FAYRE.

FOR YOUR NEAREST BREWERS FAYRE CALL [A] TALKING PAGES 0800 600 900